GINN FOR GOVERNOR

College

RUSH
CI

go
REEK

I ♥
ΔX

HANDS ACROSS THE CENTURIES

A History of the Delta Chi Fraternity
1890–2012

By Annie Miller Devoy

THE
DONNING COMPANY
PUBLISHERS

HANDS ACROSS THE CENTURIES

A History of the Delta Chi Fraternity
1890–2012

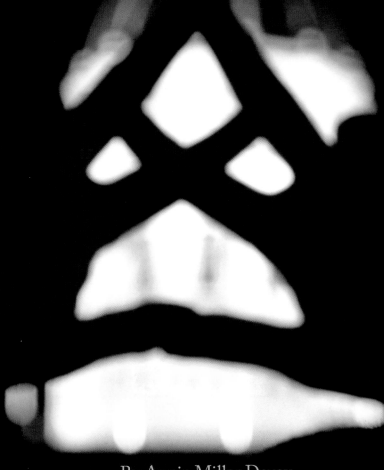

By Annie Miller Devoy

Dedicated to the Founders who dared to dream and the over 100,000 who followed them into the Bond of Brotherhood.

The Donning Company Publishers
184 Business Park Drive, Suite 206
Virginia Beach, VA 23462

Steve Mull, General Manager
Barbara Buchanan, Office Manager
Anne Burns, Editor
Scott Rule, Graphic Designer
Priscilla Odango, Imaging Artist
Tonya Washam, Marketing Specialist
Pamela Engelhard, Marketing Advisor

John Richardson, Project Director

Library of Congress Cataloging-in-Publication Data

Devoy, Annie Miller, 1967-
   Hands across the centuries : a history of the Delta Chi Fraternity, 1890-2012 / by Annie Miller Devoy.
     p. cm.
   Includes index.
   ISBN 978-1-57864-775-0
   1. Delta Chi Fraternity--History. I. Title.
   LJ75.D153D48 2012
   371.8'55--dc23

                                           2012021761

Printed in the United States of America
at Walsworth Publishing Company

TABLE OF CONTENTS

Dear Delta Chi Brothers:

At first glance, one might simply describe Delta Chi as just another of the major Greek letter fraternities. However, ever since its founding in 1890 at Cornell University, Delta Chi began building a unique heritage that has been added to by each of its 100,000+ initiates. For more than a century, Delta Chi has grown to reflect and represent the composite personal experiences and accomplishments of every one of its members and their associations together.

As a member initiated over a half century ago, Delta Chi and those I call my Brothers have provided extremely close and invaluable relationships spanning those decades. Other than family, no other tie than the bond of Delta Chi brotherhood binds more strongly in the life of an initiate. Whether an associate, new initiate or lifetime member, Delta Chi will always remain an important part of every member's human experience. From a solemn fraternal oath many years ago to my most recent e-mail, the fraternal tale unfolds with shared special occasions, weddings, births, deaths, personal successes and tragedies; all intertwined with friendships that span the ages and often many miles. It was Delta Chi's basic tenants that brought young men together without prejudice or discrimination, believing in each other and the dignity of man and a just society. It was that fraternal experience where young men learned to respect and appreciate their fellow man and find through understanding compassion and combined effort that all things can be successfully accomplished.

And so it has been a great story that a fraternity founded on the basis of justice and a close association of men could favorably impact their lives and the world they live in.........one that simply sums up the meaning and mission of Delta Chi.

In The Bond,

Brother John L. Mica
Florida '67
Member of Congress

Acknowledgments

Without the dedication and extensive knowledge of Executive Director Raymond D. Galbreth (Missouri '69) this book would not exist. His love for Delta Chi—its past, present, and future—is evident in his every conversation. I sincerely thank Ray and his wife Janet for their gracious hospitality and his gift of untold hours to this project. Delta Chi has been blessed with his leadership and loyalty. He is truly Mr. Delta Chi. The entire office staff helped in every way possible. I especially appreciate the work of Emily Audlehelm Haworth—the daughter, granddaughter, niece, and sister of Delta Chis. To her, as to all Delta Chis, this book is a story of family and tradition.

As Delta Chi continues to grow, its history will go on. If you, or your chapter, have high-resolution photographs or unique stories to share, please send them to hq@deltachi.org for preservation in the archives and possible inclusion in future projects.

It has been a pleasure learning the history of Delta Chi and a privilege to help tell your story.

Annie Miller Devoy
2012

Introduction

We sing to dear old Delta Chi, Our pride, Our guiding star, All hail to thee, O Delta Chi, Thy loving sons we are.

"The Sons of Delta Chi"
Delta Chi Songs 1912

At the 1940 Delta Chi national convention Judge Monroe Marsh Sweetland addressed his brothers. As a Founder of the fraternity, he spoke of Delta Chi since its earliest moments, not just its earliest years. At the conclusion of his remarks he invited each Delta Chi to approach and shake his hand. When the delegates were old men, Sweetland reflected, they would be standing where he was, sharing their memories and their love of Delta Chi. They would then pass on his handshake. This simple gesture, joining hands across the centuries, conveys the continuity of purpose and pride Delta Chi members have shared since 1890. Founder Sweetland would be proud to know his handshake continues to bond brothers of the past, the present, and the future.

CHAPTER ONE:

The Founding 1890–1899

A knight errant statue, prominently displayed at headquarters, echoes the ritual's themes of gallantly fighting crime, oppression, and wrong.

The Founders Of
The Delta Chi Fraternity
CORNELL UNIVERSITY   OCTOBER 13, 1890

Albert Sullard Barnes

Myron McKee Crandall

Sir Edward Coke
Spiritual Founder

John Milton Gorham

Peter Schermerhorn Johnson

Edward Richard O'Malley

Owen Lincoln Potter

Alphonse Derwin Stillman

Thomas A. Sullivan

Monroe Marsh Sweetland

Thomas David Watkins

Frederick Moore Whitney

"As I look back over the early history of our Fraternity I am impressed with the recollection of the remarkable unity and true fraternal spirit which then prevailed and had always been maintained in the parent Chapter of Delta Chi."

FOUNDER MONROE MARSH SWEETLAND

The entrance gates of Cornell, shown here in 1890, welcomed the Delta Chi Founders to campus. *Library of Congress*

Cornell University was founded in 1865 upon the belief that radical new approaches to education were necessary for the country's continued prosperity. By the late 1880s the university was solidly established as an educational pioneer encouraging new avenues of thought for its faculty and student body. Cornell was radical in several ways—it was founded with no religious affiliations, it offered coeducation from its earliest years, and it introduced an elective system allowing students to choose their own course of study. The university created a charged atmosphere of change and expansion.

It was in this fertile environment that the first seeds of Delta Chi took hold. The exact details leading up to October 13, 1890, were never entirely agreed upon. The unique perspective of each Founder, combined with the passage of years, tells a story that differs in detail but unites in the final result. No one could have imagined where the musings of these young law students in the spring of 1890 would lead.

Established in 1887, the Cornell law department charged $75 a year for three hours of law instruction a day. A high school diploma was not a prerequisite for admission and most students learned on the job as law clerks. Students of the early law school included Albert Sullard Barnes, Myron McKee Crandall, John Milton Gorham, Peter Schermerhorn Johnson, Edward Richard "E. R." O'Malley, Owen Lincoln Potter, Alphonse Derwin Stillman, Thomas A. J. Sullivan, Monroe Marsh Sweetland, Thomas David Watkins, and Frederick Moore Whitney. Politics were strategically played as law students vied for the titles of class president and law school editor of the *Cornell Daily Sun*. To Alphonse Stillman, it appeared these coveted positions routinely went to members of one small, closely-knit group, Phi Delta Phi. Stillman recalled, "I commenced agitation for an opposition to Phi Delta Phi and in a little while, us outsiders bunched somewhat like saw dust on a mill pond."

Founded at the University of Michigan Law School in 1869, the law fraternity Phi Delta Phi hit Cornell's law department in 1888 and quickly dominated the political scene. Delta Chi Founder Monroe Sweetland wrote of Phi Delta Phi in 1910, "It was during the college year 1889–90 that considerable feeling was

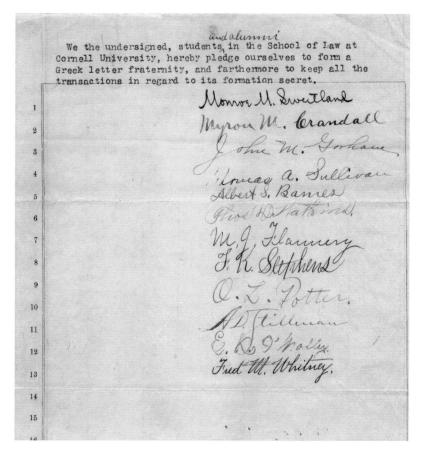

This agreement to start a fraternity, signed by all but P. S. Johnson on October 13, 1890, is a fraternity treasure. M. J. Flannery and F. K. Stephens signed the document, but dropped out early and are not considered founders.

aroused among law students not members of that fraternity because of the belief that it was attempting to control student and class politics. The antagonism to Phi Delta Phi… resulted in more or less discussion regarding the advisability of organizing for the purpose of securing full recognition in class and other college affairs." Sweetland recalls the agitation continuing into the summer months of 1890. Ongoing discussions of a new fraternity were held by some in Myron Crandall's apartment at 126 East Seneca Street in Ithaca and by others in Sweetland's law office on Wilgus Street. Sweetland and Barnes reflected many years later, "Where there is room for Delta Chi there is room for Phi Delta Phi; each will spur the other to a higher standard, to loftier ideals and to truer service to the alma mater."

Robert Heggie was the skilled Ithaca jeweler who fashioned the first two Delta Chi badges in 1890.

These men and their common desire to formally cement their association converged on the evening of October 13, 1890. In an old frame house they had rented at 315 Heustis, on the corner of Dryden Road and Heustis Street (now College Avenue), Crandall, Sweetland, Gorham, and Stillman worked out the details of the organization. According to Barnes, they presented a constitution and bylaws, which were formally adopted that October night. Sweetland recalled, "It was decided to establish at Cornell University, a Greek Letter Fraternity, with a membership confined to Law students, having in view a conservative plan of extension among other institutions of approved standing." Sweetland claimed he alone chose the name of Delta Chi, liking the way the two words sounded together, but it was most likely a group decision. According to Albert T. Wilkinson in a 1940 letter, the following men were elected to office: John M. Gorham "A", Thomas D. Watkins "B", Thomas A. J. Sullivan "C", John B. Stephens "D", and Martin J. Flannery "E". A prominent Ithaca jeweler, Robert Heggie of R. A. Heggie and Bros., produced the first two badges. Originally ordered by Barnes and Whitney, when the badges were ready Whitney could not afford his and it was purchased by Sweetland. The other Founders borrowed these badges to have their photos taken. Barnes lost his badge at a class reunion in 1915.

A committee on the ritual, composed of Stillman, Barnes, and Stephens, was appointed at the first meeting, apparently held in Sweetland's law office. Working quickly, the committee presented the ritual a week later on October 20, 1890, where it was approved.

Stillman later recalled, "I looked upon that ritual as temporary and that it would serve until some genius could devise something entirely original. The ritual contained many phrases that were not original and which, as I remember, I did not take the trouble to mark as quotations. The principal ideas are almost as old as civilization, and it was my idea that an entirely new ritual would be prepared." The ritual was rehearsed on November 14, 1890. At that meeting the name, motto, grip, and passwords were also presented for adoption.

The ritual was first performed on November 26, 1890, in the Dryden Road house, when Albert T. Wilkinson, Frank Bowman, and George Wilcox were initiated. Wilkinson later described the event, "I remember distinctly waiting on the bridge over Cascadilla gorge for some time trying to pluck up courage enough to go in and face what I expected would be a harrowing experience. As a matter of fact there was nothing to it." Wilkinson soon moved into "the house on the Hill" sharing a room with Brothers Sullivan and O'Malley. Contrary to Stillman's belief that the words he presented would ultimately be replaced, the Delta Chi initiation ritual has remained fundamentally unchanged since it was first used in November of 1890.

The Founders, as students of the law, were greatly influenced by the writings of Sir Edward Coke. Looked to as a "spiritual founder," his words and beliefs were reflected in many aspects of the new organization. Decades after throwing off the mantle of a law fraternity, Delta Chi associate members today still memorize Coke's life history and are familiar with his sayings such as, "A man's house is his castle." Within a few weeks of organization a house was procured which was used exclusively by the chapter and occupied as a home by several of the brothers. Founder Albert S. Barnes was asked in 1910 if

have been discouraged with the work, but today it is in appropriate shape for publication.   I have not issued it before for these reasons:

    1st: A book of that nature must be thoroughly up to date as to matters of facts;

    2nd: I did not deem it advisable to issue it in connection with any other fraternity publication, which would detract from its worth as a valuable book of reference.

    3d: I have hoped that one of the honorary members of New York print the book at the cost price of publication - if not almost free.   I have received [several] orders for this book, when issued, and thirty eight subscribers amounting to $19.00 have been received.

    During the winter I have established in New York City a graduate Delta Chi dining club.

    All correspondence from chapters, and relating to new chapters have been carefully placed in order by me, together with the data for catalogue and are open for inspection and corrections by the delegates.

    The ▓▓▓ regrets that not being actively engaged in the practice of law he is not in command of that corps of ▓▓▓▓ with which to pay that prompt attention to the duties of the fraternity which should be expected from him.   My shortcomings I regret and the courtesies of my fellow brothers I profoundly appreciate.

                        Yours Fraternally,

                        James Tucker.

Insert matter on next page before closing -

John Francis Tucker (NYU '96, "CC" 1896–98) presented this "CC" report in 1898. It was Tucker's visit to Cornell in the spring of 1891 that prompted the fraternity's further organization. (Esoteric titles have been blurred in the above image.)

George A. Nall (Cornell 1892) was in the earliest known photograph of Delta Chis taken in 1891.

the original intention was a purely local organization. "My answer is emphatically NO! The original minutes of the first meeting are in my hands as I write, as well as the original draft of the fraternity by-laws adopted by the meeting. The by-laws provided for the granting of charters to chapters, and the government of the Fraternity in a manner almost identical with the present plan. The first officers elected were Fraternity and not chapter officers."

On April 14, 1891, New York University student John Francis Tucker, a member of Delta Upsilon, made an historic visit to Cornell. An immediate friendship sprang up between Tucker and the Delta Chi brothers. Tucker was initiated that night and then returned to New York to establish a chapter there. Albert Wilkinson recalled Tucker's visit with great humor. "We put up a big bluff, and treated him with great formality and instructed him to return to the place whence he came and make a formal application in writing for a charter from our ancient and honorable body. As soon as he departed, there was a hurry call for a meeting to organize a body to which he could apply.…"

A governing body was organized with the following officers on April 15, 1891: Owen Potter ("AA"), John M. Gorham ("BB"), George A. Nall ("CC"), and Albert T. Wilkinson ("DD"). With Tucker's return to NYU and the establishment of their chapter of Delta Chi, the growth of the fraternity ceased to merely be the story of one chapter. Tucker continued to play

Taken in 1891, the earliest known photo of Delta Chi contains many charter members and the earliest initiates. Front row (left to right), Merton S. Gibbs ('91), Ray E. Middaugh ('92), Truman Leonard Benedict ('92), Minor Harlan Brown ('92), George Burton Wilcox ('92), and Alphonse Derwin Stillman ('91). Second row, Thomas David Watkins ('92), Frederick Moore Whitney ('91), Albert S. Barnes ('91), George A. Nall ('92), Frank P. Marquis ('91), Peter Schermerhorn Johnson ('91), and Willis Timothy Gridley ('92). Third row, Charles Sumner Lattin ('91), Thomas A. J. Sullivan ('91), Monroe Marsh Sweetland ('90), Albert T. Wilkinson ('91), Fredrick F. Bagley ('91), and Charles F. McLindon ('93). Fourth row, Owen Lincoln Potter ('90), Richard Thomas Lonergan ('92), Edward Richard O'Malley ('91), Frank Bowman ('93), and John Milton Gorham ('91).

3

Constitution

Preamble

In order to recive the advantages of an association organized for mutual assistance in the acquiring of a sound and finished legal education the Delta Chi fraternity does ordain and establish the following constitution.

Article I.

Section 1.— The name of this association shall be "The Delta Chi Fraternity," and shall consist of chapters situated at the various recognized Law Schools or colleges.

Article II.

Section 1.— Membership in the Delta Chi Fraternity shall be limited to the alumni and students in good standing in recognized Law Schools and colleges; and to such Professors of Law in such schools or colleges, and regularly licensed attorneys in good standing as may be elected to honorary membership in any chapter; and to prospective law students in good

In 1894, George A. Nall transcribed the fraternity's records. The first constitution contained the original preamble as adopted by the Founders. Odis Knight Patton (Iowa '12) wrote the current preamble in 1922.

2

Secretary's Journal

1891
April 15

A meeting of the general fra— was held on April 15th 1891, at t— rooms of its only chapter at It— New York.

A motion was duly made — carried that the constitution an— ritual in its form as read an— a whole, become the supreme instrument of the fraternity, a— take effect immediately.

By motion duly carried a committee was appointed to a suitable charter for new Messrs Potter and Stillman were the committee.

It was moved and carried proceed at once to the Election fraternity officers under the s— constitution.

The following nomination made :—
President — O. L. Potter & M. M. Sweetland.
Vice President — J. M. Gorham.
Secretary — A. S. Barnes & G. A. Nall.
Treasurer — A. T. Wilkinson.
By motion duly carried, the

The secretary's minutes from April 15, 1891, show the adoption of the constitution, ritual, and the election of fraternity officers.

HANDS ACROSS THE CENTURIES

a significant role in the early expansion of the fraternity. He recruited men not only at NYU but Dickinson Law School, Albany Law School, and the University of Minnesota. The May 1921 *Quarterly* reported that "Father Tucker," as older Delta Chis knew him, had died. Tucker was "CC" of the fraternity three times and was the editor of the first *Delta Chi Directory*.

In 1894, representatives from eight young chapters gathered in Ann Arbor for the first convention, hosted by the Michigan Chapter. Stillman's almost unchanged ritual was formally adopted at the Ann Arbor convention. The second convention was held at the Fifth Avenue Hotel in New York City on April 10–12, 1896. After electing officers, the group convened at the Hotel Jefferson for a reception and banquet.

Before the third convention, in 1897, the chapter at Buffalo had been installed as well as that of Osgoode Hall in Toronto. Convening at the Odd Fellows' Hall in Ithaca, New York, Delta Chi officially became an international fraternity. Edward C. Nettels (Chicago-Kent '00) was initiated in 1898 while a student attending the Chicago College of Law, a night school affiliated with Lake Forest University. He recalled many decades later, "When I attended a convention in 1900, the delegates there were astonished to learn that they had admitted a night law school in Chicago to membership. They said, 'We thought it was a Chapter of the Chicago University, of course.' I do

This napkin is from the first Delta Chi luncheon held on June 18, 1891. P. S. Johnson said of the napkin, "I tried to have them autograph, but everyone was too busy, so I wrote the names of those present on the one, as a souvenir."

The Fifth Avenue Hotel in New York City was the site of the 1896 and 1903 conventions.

Forrest "Buck" Hall (Michigan '96) on the far left, posed with other members of the 1895 Michigan varsity football team. *Bentley Historical Library, University of Michigan*

The March 23, 1897, minutes of the Michigan Chapter read, "Hon. Benjamin Harrison, Ex. President of the United States, admitted to honorary membership in the Michigan Chapter of Delta Chi Fraternity and instructed in the secrets of the Fraternity." *Library of Congress*

Rowing legend Fredrick D. "Freddie" Colson (Cornell '97), seated first row on the far right, was the varsity crew captain in 1897–98. A dedicated Delta Chi alumnus, Colson was a major contributor to rebuilding the Cornell Chapter house in 1902. 1898 Cornell Class Book, *Cornell University Digital Archives*

not now recall when the word Kent was added to the Chicago Chapter."

The rumblings of the law versus general fraternity debate began early in Delta Chi's history. E. G. "Count" Lorenzen, a Cornell brother referred to by A. Dix Bissell (Cornell '98, "AA" 1898–99) as the backbone of Delta Chi at the time, wrote the fraternity officers on August 27, 1898,

> I want to ask your advice upon a very delicate and important question. There are only fifty-three new law students and from these, thirty general course fraternities take the cream and the legal fraternities have to be satisfied with the rest. It is the opinion of this chapter that we cannot grow in the future unless our constitution be changed and we are allowed to go to the general course for some men, even if they are not going to be lawyers. Would it be possible to secure such a constitutional amendment, at the next convention? ...We talked to Brother Sweetland about it and, contrary to my expectations, he saw no great objection to it.

Bissell studied their request and devised a liberal interpretation of the constitution that would allow initiation if future legal studies of any sort were promised. "…A change of this character must ultimately be made to insure the future existence of Delta Chi at Cornell, and the sooner it is done the better. I am very anxious to assist the boys in this matter…" This liquid interpretation was adopted at the 1909 convention but heated discussions on the issue were not quelled. Delta Chi effectively became a general fraternity in 1922, nearly a quarter of a century after Lorenzen broached the subject.

Idle moments during Easter vacation of 1899 led to the creation of Delta Chi's first coat of arms. Brothers Roy V. Rhodes (Cornell '01) and Fraser Brown (Cornell '00) shared a room at the Mother House in Ithaca. Rhodes told the story of the coat of arms in a 1930 letter to Albert Tousley, the *Quarterly*'s editor at the time.

> One night during the Easter vacation of the year 1899, neither of us having joined the general holiday exodus from Ithaca, we were communing together over our pipes and as the conversation led into fraternity channels the idea of a coat of arms for Delta Chi was suggested. As with one accord we went to our large double desk, pulled out some paper and pencils and commenced to sketch tentative designs. Several of these were discussed, but without much accord, until we bethought ourselves of the expediency of consulting the ritual for symbols. The first reading brought about the design substantially as it now appears.

After the third convention, great emphasis was placed on internal chapter development and external growth was not vigorously pursued. The Dickinson Chapter hosted the last convention of the nineteenth century. In May 1899 delegates met in Carlisle, Pennsylvania. "From all reports the convention was given jolly good times, for none of the visiting brethren fail to gladly repeat their experiences." Granting a charter for petitioners from Syracuse University was the biggest accomplishment of note.

As they would for every global conflict to come, Delta Chi men eagerly served their country in time of need. Herman J. Westwood (Cornell '97) wrote in his quarterly report to the chapters,

"A large number of the members of our Fraternity have enlisted in the service of the United States for its war against Spain. [I have] not at hand full data as to who these men are or in what regiments they enlisted."

Precise confirmation of who was a founder and who was not a founder was debated for decades. As memories faded, stories conflicted. A campaign in the 1930s led by John B. Harshman (Ohio State '07, "AA" 1929–35) to collect information on the founding prompted a sharp response from Founder Frederick Moore Whitney. "You will probably reach the same futile result which I have reached in my voluntary efforts to do this same thing…your efforts will be just as futile as my own have been in the years since 1912 and that is nearly a quarter of a century. I am not saying this to discourage you but it amuses me to think that Brother Harshman has requested anybody at this date to get together any data regarding the founding of the fraternity…" The details may be fuzzy but the intentions and results are undisputed. In 1890, Delta Chi was just an idea in the minds of friends. A mere decade later it had firmly defined itself and was spreading across not only the country, but the continent.

The delegates took time to pose during the 1903 New York convention.

HANDS ACROSS THE CENTURIES

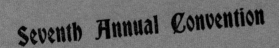

Harrison "Boss" Weeks (Michigan '02) was the quarterback of the 1901 Michigan Wolverines "Point-a-Minute" team.

By the turn of the century Delta Chi had grown to ten chapters. The brothers continued to convene annually with great enthusiasm. The sixth convention, held in 1900, met in New York City. Thirty-one delegates and alternates were in attendance. The convention went smoothly despite the unexpected resignation of Mark H. Irish as "AA" in January of 1900. A. J. Feight, "BB", took up where Irish left off and business continued as usual. Edward C. Nettels (Chicago-Kent '00, "AA" 1904–05) remembered attending the 1900 convention as a delegate. "My Chapter very generously voted me $25 for expenses, which for the week I was there barely paid for a room, not considering food and drinks."

During the first decade, the fraternity's earliest members facilitated intra-chapter communication beyond conventions. The Founders' frequent visits and active involvement was the organization's glue. As time passed, however, the earliest members lost touch with Delta Chi. Without their guidance, the group was at risk of faltering.

The Cornell House Fire

The decade began tragically for the mother chapter at Cornell. On January 29, 1900, the fraternity house on Heustis Street in Ithaca was destroyed by fire. One brother recalled:

The original Cornell Chapter house at 315 Heustis Street was the site of a fatal fire in January of 1900.

Sunday evening January 28, 1900 all the boys were in and the lights were out early. About half-past five on the morning of the 29th we were awakened by the cry of fire coming from the hall on the third floor. The house was so arranged that the study rooms were on the first and second floors, which were connected with both a rear and front stairway. The dormitories were off from a hallway on the third floor, and connected with the other floors by only one stairway...Robert Congdon and Neil Andrews luckily had left their door open, and were awakened by the light of the fire shining in upon them. They immediately gave the alarm and awakened us all. When the fire was discovered the stairway was a mass of flames and the only way to reach the ground was by jumping from the windows on the third floor. Ten of the boys jumped from the front windows to the roof of the front porch, and then to the ground...The four remaining boys were unable to reach the windows over the porch and had to jump the whole distance. All of them were severely injured. The weather was extremely cold and the injured were carried to neighboring houses and cared for as well as could be, until the ambulance arrived and they were carried to the Infirmary.

The *New York Times* reported on the most seriously injured men including John F. Lonergan from Albany, New York. His injuries were listed as a "broken nose, compound fracture of the thigh and broken arm." Lonergan's mother and sister reached Ithaca by train in time to be at his bedside when he died from his injuries. John Lonergan's watch was later found among the house ruins and was returned to his family in Albany.

The chapter house and its contents were totally destroyed with the exception of the library. An insurance payment of $900 was received. Alumni met as quickly as February 3 in New York City to discuss the tragedy. A committee was assembled to procure a new home for the Cornell brothers. Members included William M. McCrea ('00, Cornell "A" at the time of the tragedy), James O'Malley ('01), Floyd L Carlisle ('03), and S. Edwin Banks ('95). With the generous support of active members and alumni, the chapter bought and extensively renovated the Alpha Delta Phi Lodge on East Buffalo Street. Built in 1879, the house was said to be the first building in America built solely for fraternity purposes. The Cornell boys would occupy this house until 1912.

The 1902 convention, Delta Chi's eighth, was held in Chicago.

The need for a fraternity publication was discussed at the eighth annual convention, held at the Grand Pacific Hotel in Chicago in July 1902. The *Delta Chi Quarterly* name was adopted and a seemingly simple production plan was put into place. This plan proposed the appointment of an editor and business manager, appeals for alumni subscriptions, and the sale of advertisement to cover all expenses. A letter from Brother James P. Magenis summed up the thoughts of most, "As a member of Delta Chi…I want to cordially commend your enterprise in beginning a publication in the interests of the Fraternity. Nothing will so bind the boys together, nothing will so enlighten them as to matters important to our well-being, nothing will so awaken an interest as some

form of periodical." More than the delegates' enthusiasm, however, was required to make the publication a reality. It was quickly realized that the 1899 catalogue of alumni members was hopelessly out of date. Without a working list of alumni, the men took a different approach and in 1903 the constitution was amended to make every undergraduate Delta Chi a subscriber upon payment of his annual dues. This assured a subscription list of nearly 250 men. At the subscription cost of $0.50 a year, the first *Quarterly* was printed in April of 1903. The editors announced, "…with the usual temerity of the novitiate editor, and with fraternal greetings, we present to the readers Volume One, Number One of the *Delta Chi Quarterly*."

The 1903 convention met in the luxurious Fifth Avenue Hotel in New York City. George Ade's satirical Broadway production *The Sultan of Sulu* was on the agenda for the evening of Friday, April 17. A brother reported, "The first two rows of the orchestra were reserved for us and we had an excellent opportunity to see a most enjoyable opera. The New York chapters appeared to have initiated the Honorable Mr. Kiram, governor of the Island of Sulu, for above the executive mansion floated the well know Delta Chi banner." Delegates toured the city and lavishly dined between work sessions. In what resembles an early form of Twitter, delegates at the convention were asked to make speeches of only twenty words in length at the closing banquet. One delegate used his word quota exactly by saying, "I came to the convention to represent my chapter and to have a good time. I had a good time."

The fraternity focused largely on its internal policies during this time adopting a policy of conservative expansion. Founded as a professional law fraternity, Delta Chi routinely initiated members of general fraternities. As the fraternity expanded, opinions on this diverged. Some chapters voluntarily refrained from "dual membership" and they pushed for consistency on the issue through constitutional change. Elected "CC" at the 1903 convention, Floyd Carlisle (Cornell '03) took hold of the single membership debate. A popular and charismatic student leader, Carlisle was Cornell class president in both his sophomore and senior years. He championed a change in Delta Chi's form of government that would weaken the fraternity's acceptance of dual membership. E. J. Woodhouse (Virginia '07) wrote, "Sooner or later this question of double fraternity allegiance must be settled by Delta Chi, and the sooner the better."

Delegates to the 1903 convention in New York City enjoyed a standing room only performance of George Ade's *The Sultan of Sulu*.

A 1903 *Quarterly* made reference to some of the most active Delta Chis of the era. Brothers Dunn and Cummings of the Union Chapter visited the Georgetown Chapter in their "fine house at 1629 Q Street, N.W." Brothers Bride and Kearns acted as tour guides.

HANDS ACROSS THE CENTURIES

In 2000 the *Quarterly* paid tribute to the tradition of Delta Chi music.

THE MUSIC OF DELTA CHI

DELEGATES AT THE 1903 CONVENTION RECOGNIZED THE IMPORT OF MUSIC IN THE LIFE OF A FRATERNITY. BROTHER HARRY HYDE BARNUM (CHICAGO-KENT '03) WAS APPOINTED CHAIRMAN OF THE NEWLY FORMED MUSIC COMMITTEE. "EVERY DELTA CHI, WHETHER HE BE ALUMNUS OR UNDERGRADUATE WILL, UPON A LITTLE SERIOUS REFLECTION, REALIZE THE IMPORTANCE OF PRESERVING AND ENLARGING THE COLLECTION OF OUR FRATERNITY MUSIC." BARNUM REPORTED THE MICHIGAN CHAPTER WHISTLE HAD BEEN FORMALLY ADOPTED AS THE FRATERNITY'S WHISTLE. SONGS COLLECTED BY BARNUM INCLUDED "COMRADES WHEN I'M NO MORE DRINKING," "HAPPY DELTA CHIS," AND "TOAST TO DELTA CHI." "LET EVERYBODY WITH ANY TALENT IN THIS DIRECTION GET TO WORK. IF YOU CAN'T WRITE WORDS, WRITE MUSIC; A WALTZ, FOR EXAMPLE, OR SET THE DELTA CHI YELL TO MUSIC...AMONG US MANY MEMBERS, DELTA CHI MUST HAVE MANY POETS AND MUSICIANS. LET US HEAR FROM THEM. WILL YOU HELP?" BARNUM'S PLEA LED TO A FLURRY OF COMPOSITIONS INCLUDING "BAUM'S TOAST TO DELTA CHI," F. J. BAUM (CHICAGO '08); "BRANDT'S TOAST TO DELTA CHI," A. W. BRANDT (MICHIGAN '10); "THE FRAT I LOVE," W. W. BRIDE (GEORGETOWN '04); AND SEVERAL SELECTIONS BY FOUNDER PETER SCHERMERHORN JOHNSON, "DELTA CHI, HURRAH, HURRAH!" AND "FOVENS MATER."

HERMAN J. WESTWOOD (CORNELL '97) TOOK UP THE TASK OF COMPILING THE DELTA CHI MUSIC. IN MARCH 1912 HE PUBLISHED A PERMANENT SONGBOOK OF THE FRATERNITY. A SECOND EDITION WAS PUBLISHED IN 1925 UNDER THE DIRECTION OF THE KANSAS CHAPTER WHO FOUND "THAT SINGING AT THE TABLE AND AROUND THE PIANO HAS BEEN ONE OF THE GREATEST AIDS IN DEVELOPING INTERNAL HARMONY THAT WE HAVE HAD." THE SONGBOOK COMMITTEE URGED ALL TO BUY A COPY, FOR ONE DOLLAR EACH, BY SAYING, "A SINGING CHAPTER IS ALWAYS A HAPPY ONE."

THE MAY 1933 *QUARTERLY* WAS THE NEXT SONGBOOK PUBLISHED AND CONTAINED TWENTY TUNES. A NEWER EDITION WAS NOT PUBLISHED UNTIL 1946 AND AFTER THAT IT WAS 1965. THE CENTENNIAL EDITION OF THE *CORNERSTONE* CONTAINED SEVEN OF THE OLD SONGS INCLUDING A CENTENNIAL VERSE TO THE "BOND SONG," WRITTEN BY MARIAN HAMMERT, WIFE OF FRED HAMMERT (OKLAHOMA '60, "AA" 1985–87). "AS JOYOUSLY WE RAISE OUR GLASSES, TO TOAST OUR FOUNDING AT CORNELL, WE FOREVER WILL REMEMBER, OUR BROTHERS IN THE BOND TO TELL, THE CENTURY OF OUR PROUD TRADITIONS."

Sixteen chapters were represented at the 1904 convention where a new form of government was adopted. A governing board of fifteen men, termed the "XX", was created. From this group of fifteen the offices of "AA", "CC", and "DD" were filled. After 1904 the offices of "BB" and "EE" were discontinued. From 1904 on members of the "XX", other than the officers, were known as "BBs". Convention delegates gathered for meetings and entertainment at the mother chapter in Ithaca. "It is the plan of the committee to instill into all visiting delegates the idea and advantages of a chapter house." The question of making chapter houses mandatory was discussed with great interest. The Georgetown Chapter was very proud of their house and, like most fraternities of the time, engaged a butler. The Georgetown butler, Clarence, told a story enjoyed by all Delta Chis. On his first day, in his freshly pressed white coat, Clarence eagerly answered the doorbell. "Who is living in this house?" the mailman asked. "They told me, but I forgot," Clarence responded. "I think it's called the 'Delicate Child House.'"

The Georgetown Chapter hosted a prestigious event on February 24, 1904, when the Honorable William Jennings Bryan made a special trip to be initiated as a Delta Chi. Bryan, three-time candidate for president of the United States and a dominant force in the liberal wing of the Democratic Party, was led blindfolded into the inner realm "and soon Col. Bryan came forth as Brother Bryan and Delta Chi was honored." In attendance that evening was Gonzalo de Quesada, Georgetown alumnus and the Cuban minister to the United States. The *Quarterly* reported, "It would have done the heart of any loyal Delta Chi good to have witnessed the greetings between Brothers Bryan and Quesada. They are old time friends and greeted each other affectionately for the first time as brothers in Delta Chi."

William Jennings Bryan (above) and Gonzalo de Quesada (below) shared the Delta Chi grip on February 24, 1904, the night of Bryan's Georgetown initiation. *Library of Congress*

President Teddy Roosevelt, left, posed with Vice President Charles W. Fairbanks, who was a Delta Chi brother, in 1904. *Library of Congress*

The 1905 governing board of the fraternity included, bottom row, Rufus G. Shirley (NYU '02), Edward C. Nettels (Chicago-Kent '00), A. Frank John (Dickinson '00), and Hugh R. Fullerton (Michigan '04). Middle row, John J. Kuhn (Cornell '98), William W. Bride (Georgetown '04), Russell Wiles (Northwestern '04), Fredrick Dickinson (Chicago '05), and Floyd L. Carlisle (Cornell '03). Top row, LeRoy T. Harkness (NYU '03), James O'Malley (Cornell '02), Harry H. Barnum (Chicago-Kent '03), and Norman H. Smith (Michigan '05).

At the turn of the century alumni chapters were quite committed. Members of the Chicago Alumni Chapter found they were "imbued with fresh enthusiasm, vigor and fraternal spirit by association with members of the active chapters." With dues set at one dollar per year, the chapter had smokers and dinners at least once a month with the average attendance being thirty-five brothers. The New York Alumni Chapter, active since its formation in 1894, had been modeled to be a miniature bar association. Only brothers who had graduated from law school and who were members of the bar were eligible for admission. The 1903 convention delegates recognized that many Delta Chis who studied law later abandoned it. Alumni chapters applying for charters were given a clear directive. "Any Delta Chi, not a member of an undergraduate chapter, whether or not a graduate or a lawyer, should be eligible to membership." This sentiment would help pave the way for the later general membership debate.

Representatives from every chapter, with one exception, made the trip to Toronto, Canada, in June 1905 demonstrating the truly international nature of the fraternity. Osgoode Hall brothers hosted the delegates at the King Edward Hotel. One attendee recalled, "This convention was remarkable for the wonderful hospitality shown by our Canadian brethren." Petitions for charter were not considered lightly. The ranks of Delta Chi were denied applications from Yale and Boston University, as well as the Universities of Maine, Cincinnati, and Colorado. "A Delta Chi charter is no longer to be had for the mere asking. Petitioning bodies must hereafter be qualified not only as regards the personnel of their members. They must represent institutions which offer conditions and opportunities commensurate with the policies and possibilities of the Fraternity." In a show of great geographical expansion, an application from Leland Stanford Jr. University was approved as well as the University of Virginia. At the close

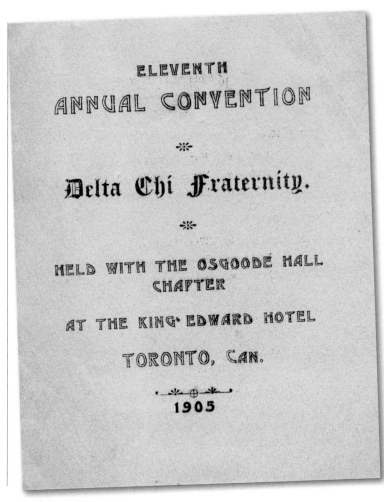

ELEVENTH ANNUAL CONVENTION

Delta Chi Fraternity.

HELD WITH THE OSGOODE HALL CHAPTER

AT THE KING EDWARD HOTEL

TORONTO, CAN.

1905

The 1905 convention delegates gathered in Toronto.

Annual Convention
OF THE
Delta Chi Fraternity
TO BE HELD AT

Ann Arbor, Michigan, June 21-22-23, 1906

Program

THURSDAY, JUNE 21

2:00 P. M. Opening business meeting at Cook House.
4:00 P. M. Coaching Party to Whitmore Lake.
7:30 P. M. Dinner, smoke talk, etc., Whitmore Lake.

FRIDAY, JUNE 22

9:30 A. M. Business meeting, Cook House.
2:00 P. M. Business meeting, Cook House.
5:00 P. M. Trolley ride to Michigan Center.
7:30 P. M. Dinner at the Dew Drop Inn.

SATURDAY, JUNE 23

9:30 A. M. Business meeting, Cook House.
2:00 P. M. Closing business meeting, Cook House.
4:00 P. M. Walks and drives about town.
8:30 P. M. Banquet at Cook House.

Accommodations may be had by writing the Cook House, Ann Arbor, Michigan, not later than June 15. Cook House Rates on American Plan from $2 to $3 per day.

The banquet will be served in the banqueting hall of the Cook House on Saturday, June 23, at 8:30 o'clock. Price per plate $3.00.

All Brothers desiring to attend please fill out and mail the enclosed blank at your earliest convenience. Please address your replies to

CHAS. B. CARTER, Chairman,
Delta Chi House,
Ann Arbor, Mich.

After their reception at the White House, delegates to the thirteenth annual convention in 1907 dined in one of Washington, D.C.'s most popular restaurants of the time, Harvey's Oyster House. *Library of Congress*

of the convention one brother told the assembly, "There is no United States, no England, no Canada, nothing as I can see but Delta Chi."

Convention delegates returned to Ann Arbor in June 1906. Two of the officers elected would immeasurably impact the fraternity. "AA" John J. Kuhn (Cornell '98) and "CC" William W. "Billy" Bride (Georgetown '04) were familiar faces at chapter houses across the country in the many years to come. The induction of new chapters was no mundane affair, as Billy Bride remarked in the May 1907 *Quarterly*. He detailed the bill of fare from the April 13, 1907, Texas Chapter installation. The menu included martini cocktails, caviar on toast, tenderloin, trout, spring chicken, French peas, asparagus on toast, and Louis Roederer champagne. Bride concluded, "A new born babe, a lusty, vigorous son was born to Delta Chi. As an installing officer, I can only say, as a message to the fraternity, that both mother and son are doing well."

A representative from every active chapter, along with more than one hundred actives and alumni, met in Washington, D.C., for the largest gathering Delta Chi had ever seen. A highlight of the thirteenth annual convention was a formal reception held at the White House with President Teddy Roosevelt. The delegates' schedule read, "April 2nd, 1907, 2:15 to 2:45, reception by President Roosevelt in the East Room of the White House." Distinguished Delta Chis attending the reception included Vice President Charles W. Fairbanks, Secretary George B. Cortelyou, Congressmen Bennett and Harding, and Cuban Minister Gonzalo de Quesada. Fairbanks was an honorary Delta Chi from the Michigan Chapter. Upon the Roosevelt-Fairbanks election in 1904, Brother Rufus G. Shirley ("DD") wrote to Fairbanks, "I write you this letter so that you may know that the entire Fraternity congratulates you most heartily on the recent victory which you so largely contributed to secure in the late political campaign."

The role of the *Quarterly* was sharply defined during the 1907 convention. The committee on fraternity publications dictated that "...the *Quarterly* consist principally of articles on the various Chapters, news items from Chapters and their Alumni, with the usual departments of Chapter Correspondence, Alumni Notes, Among the Greeks, etc." The committee further recommended, "...no legal articles appear, except those of unusual merit or interest." The completed *Delta Chi Directory* showed a total living membership of 2,172. Alumni continued to contribute amusing anecdotes like the note of John J. Kuhn and William S. Peace (Cornell '98 and '94). "Johnnie informed us that they took a course in music and art in Paris, sang Delta Chi songs in every town they visited, and that Bill was sober on September 24th."

Brother George B. Cortelyou (Georgetown) was President McKinley's personal secretary and was at his side when an assassin took his mark. As McKinley lay dying, his last words were, "My wife – be careful, Cortelyou, how you tell her." *Library of Congress*

The 1907 convention delegates can all be found in this *Quarterly* picture titled "Knights Errant."

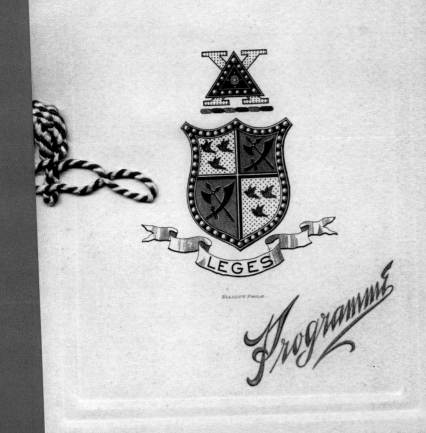

The 1907 delegates met in Washington, D.C.

Programme

Monday, April 1st

FIRST SESSION

Address of Welcome to the City, Hon. H. L. West
Response on behalf of the Fraternity, John J. Kuhn, "AA"
Response on behalf of the Alumni, L. Barton Case
Response on behalf of Active Chapters, W. W. Taylor

12:30 to 1 o'clock—LUNCH AT THE CHAPTER HOUSE

1 to 3 o'clock—SECOND SESSION

3 to 5 o'clock—AUTOMOBILE TRIP ALL-AROUND WASHINGTON

8 o'clock—SMOKER AT THE UNIVERSITY CLUB

Tuesday, April 2d

10 to 12 o'clock—THIRD SESSION

12 to 12:30 o'clock—LUNCH AT THE CHAPTER HOUSE

12:30 to 2 o'clock—FOURTH SESSION

2:30 o'clock—RECEPTION AT WHITE HOUSE BY PRESIDENT ROOSEVELT

3:00 o'clock—CONVENTION PHOTOGRAPH ON STEPS OF TREASURY DEPARTMENT

4:00 o'clock—BASE BALL GAME, YALE VS. GEORGETOWN, AT GEORGETOWN FIELD

8:30 o'clock—SMOKER AND INITIATION AT THE CHAPTER HOUSE

Wednesday, April 3d

10 to 12:30 o'clock—FIFTH SESSION

12:30 to 1 o'clock—LUNCH AT THE CHAPTER HOUSE

1:00 o'clock—SIXTH SESSION

8:30 o'clock—BANQUET AT HOTEL RALEIGH

Founder E. R. O'Malley (Cornell) was elected New York attorney general in 1908 and served as a New York State Supreme Court justice from 1925 until 1933. Teddy Roosevelt remarked, "Mr. O'Malley is a mighty fine exhibit of good citizenship and has made a good record." *Library of Congress*

While the serious debates of the fraternity are well recorded, it cannot be forgotten that since its earliest years Delta Chis came together for a great deal of fun. The Minnesota Chapter described their celebration of New Year's Eve 1908, "…Those of us who were in town, together with our ladies, indulged in a coasting party…The hill was in elegant condition for coasting, and Brother Case guided the bob with such skill that the ladies were not alarmed by the precipitous banks on either side. Later we went to the house and pulled candy and watched the old year out." There is no doubt that fun was had in chapter houses and convention gatherings alike. One report of the 1908 convention read,

"Here Johnny Kuhn and Joe Hartigan were seen in a new role. Clad in the regulation white vests and armed with towels they took the orders and dispensed the drinks with the precision and regularity of bona fide chemists. Their strongest feature was their regularity. They made a few trifling mistakes, such as putting pepper sauce in the place of bitters, but on the while their service was excellent."

As the fraternity aged, its alumni inevitably did as well. The *Quarterly* more frequently published death notices as well as the happier occasions of marriages and births. The March 1906 *Quarterly*, Vol. 4, No. 1, reported, "C. Moran Barry is the

The early decades of Delta Chi were scattered with professional baseball players. Their brothers kept close track of their careers, reporting on them faithfully to the *Quarterly*. Edward B. "Ed" Kenna (West Virginia '02), son of United States Senator John E. Kenna, was known in professional baseball circles as the "Pitching Poet." Kenna was the second-string pitcher for the Philadelphia Athletics in 1902. They won the American League Championship that year with a record of eighty-three wins and fifty-three losses. Baseball historian Rex Hamann wrote of Kenna, "Amidst a rough and tumble throng of players who occupied mainly blue collar professions, Kenna was a sort of flower in the pasture."

The "Pitching Poet" Ed Kenna (West Virginia '02) is fourth from the left on the top row of this 1902 Philadelphia Athletics' team photo. *Photo by Oscar Winter, Philadelphia, Pennsylvania*

Another brother, Harry Lee Spratt (Virginia '12), made great contributions to Delta Chi's inter-fraternity record before joining the Boston Nationals as shortstop. The June 1911 *Quarterly* reported, "In the inter-fraternity baseball series Delta Chi defeated Sigma Nu 9-0 and we expect to be equally as fortunate in the remaining games..."

Leftfielder Arthur H. "Art" Bader (Washington University '09) began his career in the American League playing for the St. Louis Browns. He left the majors and played for the Pueblo Indians and the Des Moines Boosters. The December 1910 *Quarterly* reported that Bader "has retired from baseball. During the season of 1909 he was hit on the head by a pitched ball and seriously injured, and has not entirely gotten over the effects of it. Baseball lost a star of the first magnitude when he retired."

The University of Virginia formed a unique relationship with baseball in the summer of 1913 and called upon its fraternities for help. The Washington Senators, training in Charlottesville for the summer, were unable to find suitable hotel accommodations. Delta Chi came to the rescue and gave up their house for the big leaguers. The *Binghampton Press*, March 13, 1913, wrote, "It was one of the neatest compliments ever paid by college baseball enthusiasts to the professional exponents of the game."

The early Delta Chi ball players would surely have cheered when Brother Jon Daniels (Cornell 1999) was named Major League Baseball's youngest general manager in history. Daniels took control of the Texas Rangers in 2006 at the age of twenty-eight.

SPRATT-BOSTON-NAT.

Harry Lee Spratt (Virginia '12) played shortstop, second base, and center field for the Boston Braves in 1911 and 1912. *American Tobacco Company*

very proud father of a little daughter. She is the first baby of the Georgetown Chapter." The diversity of the brotherhood was reflected in alumni occupations, which went well beyond the practice of law. Even founder and author of the ritual, Alphonse D. Stillman (Cornell '91) left his law practice to take up farming. The Reverend Robert Davis (New York Law '05) was believed to be the first Delta Chi member of the clergy. Edward J. Woodhouse (Virginia '07) was an assistant librarian at the United States Supreme Court Library. Charles W. Casey (Washington '05) was in charge of the foreign collections of Anheuser Busch. His address was simply "The Brewery, St. Louis." Three of the national parks' most famous lodges, Mammoth Hotel, the Fountain Hotel, and the Old Faithful Inn, were all managed by Delta Chis, recognizable to brothers passing through by their proudly worn lapel pins.

The issue of single versus dual membership reached a fever pitch during the 1908 convention. One brother recalled of the 1908 gathering, "A long and hard battle was waged by the adherents of the single fraternity movement, and they nearly succeeded in having such an amendment passed, a mere margin of two votes out of sixty-three prevented its passage." The issue would be revisited and resolved at the next year's gathering, the fifteenth annual convention. A determined group of Delta Chis gathered in Ithaca for the first three days of April 1909. This convention resolved to put the single fraternity membership question to rest. It was determined that in the future no members of general fraternities would be eligible for Delta Chi membership. The actions of the convention were severely scrutinized by H. H. Barnum ("AA" 1907–08). Three delegates who were not supporting single membership were unseated for various alleged offences. After the voting was complete, and single membership had passed, the delegates were reseated. In a letter to Billy Bride, Barnum passionately wrote, "…the action taken by the convention in unseating delegates for various minor offences was a mere pretext and was absolutely unwarranted not only by our constitution but by all sense of decency and justice. The tactics were those which no political convention would descend to without shame… A legal fraternity should have higher ideals than to descend to such trickery and no good can possibly come of action so inherently rotten."

The Delta Chi whistle and response were adopted in 1909 at the fraternity's fifteenth annual convention.

This maneuvering ultimately cost Delta Chi the chapters at New York Law, Northwestern, Washington University in St. Louis, and West Virginia. They voluntarily returned their charters, questioning the convention's unseating and believing that they could not live up to the standards of the fraternity at large.

Concessions were made allowing chapters time to transition away from the dual membership practices of the past. By the sixteenth convention, progress was reported under the new regulations and chapters generally felt they were better off due to the change. The Virginia group reported in 1910, "It has been a complete success and Delta Chi at Virginia is stronger than she ever was." The issue of becoming a general fraternity was hinted at in Chicago's chapter correspondence. Considering their rival law fraternities Phi Delta Phi and Phi Alpha Delta, Chicago commented, "Our rushing season has been quite spirited this year as the enrollment in the Law School is small to support three fraternities. However, the new men are a fine bunch of fellows…We have the quality even if we have not the quantity." A Virginia brother, E. J. Woodhouse, reported to the *Quarterly*, "A Phi Delta Phi, who is also a general fraternity man, remarked to the writer today, 'You carry on Delta Chi like a general fraternity, don't you?' We are glad that such an impression is abroad." The general fraternity

The Stanford Chapter was active from 1905 until 1970.

HANDS ACROSS THE CENTURIES

issue would not be seriously addressed for another ten years.

An exemplification of the handshake ritual was performed on April 1, 1909, in the Cornell Chapter house. Hugh VanNest Bodine was the evening's initiate. A number of older brothers were present to witness the ceremony including Albert T. Wilkinson. The May 1909 *Quarterly* reported, "...not the least interesting thing that occurred was the clasping of hands in fraternity of Brother Albert T. Wilkinson, the first initiate into the fraternity, and Brother Bodine the last one." The bond of brotherhood would carry Delta Chi confidently into the next decade.

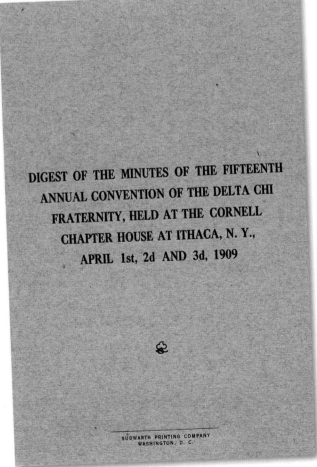

DIGEST OF THE MINUTES OF THE FIFTEENTH ANNUAL CONVENTION OF THE DELTA CHI FRATERNITY, HELD AT THE CORNELL CHAPTER HOUSE AT ITHACA, N. Y., APRIL 1st, 2d AND 3d, 1909

SUDWARTH PRINTING COMPANY
WASHINGTON, D. C.

CHAPTER THREE

1910–1919

Billy Bride compiled and published a Delta Chi directory in time for the fraternity's twentieth anniversary in 1910.

NEW Delta Chi Directory

complete and up-to-date.

1890 ❧ ❧ 1910

Compiled and edited by W. W. Bride, "CC." Pocket size, bound in flexible leather, contains names and addresses of practically every living member of the Fraternity. Geographical and alphabetical index. Invaluable. *$1.00 - - - postpaid.*

Every Lawyer and Delta Chi should have one.

W.W. Bride, "CC"

Century Building, Washington, D.C.

The February 1910 *Quarterly* featured some of the chapter houses.

"Delta Chi reminds me of a wheel. The ten of us combined were the hub. Now the wheel has twenty-two strong spokes and we of 1890 are standing on the ever-expanding circumference."

FOUNDER ALBERT S. BARNES (CORNELL '91)

The sixteenth convention met in Columbus, Ohio, in April 1910. The Southern Hotel, with a rate of $2.25 a night, served as convention headquarters. A reception committee met the trains at Union Depot making themselves recognizable to visiting delegates by sporting white carnations in their lapels. Edward Warner Wright (Osgoode Hall '08) became the fraternity's second Canadian "AA", the first being Mark Irish (Osgoode Hall 1897, "AA" 1899–1900). The June 1910 *Quarterly* reported, "Old friendships were renewed and new ones formed with true Delta Chi zeal." The Michigan official pin was adopted by this convention as the official badge. It retailed for $5.00.

The seventeenth Delta Chi convention banquet was held in Chicago on July 15, 1911.

This picture of the 1911 convention attendees includes at least six of the early "AAs"—John Harshman, A. Frank John, Edward C. Nettels, William W. Bride, Harry Hyde Barnum, and Henry V. McGurren.

The T Association, still a vital part of the University of Texas Athletic Department, was founded in 1912 by a group of Texas Delta Chi varsity athletes. Founders, pictured from left to right, were Demps Bland, K. Krahl, Grady Niblo, and Morgan Vining. The fifth Founder, not pictured, was Steve Pinckney.

By 1911 there had been over three thousand men initiated into the brotherhood of Delta Chi. Every Delta Chi chapter, save one, entered the fraternity's third decade occupying a chapter house. These houses were the heart and soul of fraternity life. The Virginia brothers were delighted to report, "There has been added a pool table to the chapter's personality, a thing of beauty and utility, and thousands of times do the balls click during the day, and sometimes even unto twelve at night…Over its green surface Delta Chi meets Delta Chi many times a week."

Billy Bride urged alumni to attend conventions. "Come swell the attendance and catch the habit. It is the habit that you will want to grow with the years. I have attended seven conventions and I know." While gathering in Chicago for the seventeenth convention, delegates attended a Chicago White Sox and Boston Nationals game. Fellow Delta Chi Harry Lee Spratt was shortstop for Boston at the time. "It was some game," George H. Kaercher remembered. "The writer has no idea what the score was

and hereby challenges any Delt to remember. But he does know all about the five Deltas on either side of him and the antics of those in front of him." Increasing convention attendance and general growth were working topics of the convention. Regarding growth, the *Quarterly* reported Harry Hageman and Dennis Lyons (both Minnesota '00) each welcomed the arrival of baby daughters. "Girls aren't going to help us any. Try again boys."

As the Cornell Chapter learned after its fatal fire, the loss of a Delta Chi while in the company of his brothers is especially painful. Georgetown reported in the October 1911 *Quarterly*, "At twilight on the evening of July 3, while bathing in the Potomac River at a beach on the Virginia shore about a mile west of the national capitol, John Edwin Holliday, 'A' of the Georgetown Chapter 1910–11, was accidentally drowned a few yards from three fraternity brothers and within view of the University that had witnessed the richest moments of his red-blooded life." The chapter mourned but rallied for rush that fall and was proud of their new home. "The fellows are going to work with an enthusiasm and intensity of interest, which speaks well for our future. Our New Home, which is one of the most splendid and commodious in College, is being attractively furnished and we are ready to begin a campaign, which promises great things for Delta Chi."

California brothers of the era had their mothers to thank for the comforts of their new home. "Those ever-sacrificing mothers of ours have been meeting once a week planning how they may aid us in making the new Chapter House comfortable to live in, in those little ways where a woman's touch alone can satisfy even the most unobserving man." Dickinson brothers moved around this time as well but kept their alumni in mind. "Our old lease expired April first [1912]

Fred Carpenter: The President's Right-hand Man

Fred W. Carpenter (Minnesota '97) left his position of stenographer in a San Francisco law office to join William Howard Taft as his personal secretary in 1900. Judge Taft was preparing to leave for the Philippines as head of the civil commission. Carpenter stayed by Taft's side through his service as governor of the Philippines, United States secretary of war, and eventually as president of the United States. The July 25, 1908, *Chicago-Tribune* reported on Carpenter: "Mr. Carpenter is about as much of a physical contrast to his chief as one well could imagine. He is slender, and entirely lacking in sturdy physique. He has a softness and gentleness about his actions which disarm everyone, but he has learned the trick...of acting as a sieve through which only the important things and persons really worth while succeed in reaching the big man, for whom he labors so persistently and so successfully."

In 1909 Carpenter worked in his White House office. *Library of Congress*

Washington brothers celebrated Founders' Day in 1915 with three days of events.

and we decided to re-lease our old house but in the meantime we were unusually fortunate in securing a large commodious brick house with fifteen rooms and two baths…We had the old lock transferred to the new house so that the old alumni can use their keys when they come back. This is the original lock that was used on the rooms when the chapter was founded nineteen years ago."

Filled with the successes of their collegiate days, many Delta Chis fearlessly stepped out into the world. The *Quarterly* reported on the attempts of W. E. R. Kemp (Washington University '09) to secure employment with J.P. Morgan & Company. "He insisted upon seeing Mr. Morgan personally and after several days of determined efforts while the guardian of the outer chamber was away he gained an entrance. The great financial king was busily engaging in solving some problem when Kemp marched in, coughed, bowed, extended a card, and throwing out his chest, exclaimed, 'I am W.E.R. Kemp from St. Louis. Just thought I would come over and assist you in some matters.' The other did not look up or answer but continued with his problem. Kemp coughed rather loudly…'All right,' was the answer, 'begin with the cuspidors and follow up with the windows and hurry. My counsel is expected any minute.'"

Founders' Day was celebrated universally but often in ways unique to each chapter. Stanford's 1912 invitation to gather at Levy's Tavern in Los Angeles read, "Founders' Day-October 13- is Sunday. Come ye now and indulge in the heathenish Hot-Bed of Hegemonic Hemeralpia and Dare-Devil Daldalian, Deleterious, Deadly Delta Chi Spirits." Delegates compared their Founders' Day traditions when they met in Toronto for the 1913 convention. This convention was the first held since the 1911 decision to convene biannually. The event garnered such attention a special edition of the *Toronto Daily Brief* was published. The front page was dedicated to Delta Chi with the headline screaming, "Great Sensation, Delta Chi Fraternity Meets Here." The article went on to name the convention as "the most important international gathering ever held in Toronto." The work of the convention illustrated the significant expansion of the fraternity. The 1913 election of the "XX" was notable because for the first time, no chapter had more than one "XX" member. Geographically, the "XX" membership was more widely scattered than ever. The first member from the Pacific Coast came in 1911;

A 1913 University of California publication reported, "Terror, the pedigreed bull terrier of the Delta Chis, completed the final round of the Inter-fraternity Dog Fight Series by cleaning up Barry, the former undisputed campus champion who resides at the Sigma Nu house."

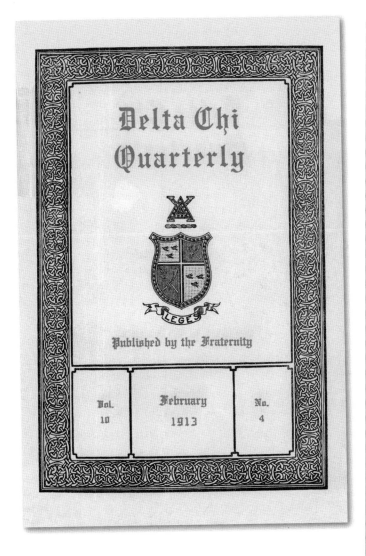

Delta Chi Quarterly

Published by the Fraternity

| Vol. 10 | February 1913 | No. 4 |

George B. Bush (Stanford '10), the fraternity's first traveling secretary, sent a postcard of the new Cornell Chapter house to Pierson W. Banning (Chicago-Kent '10) in 1915. Completed in 1913, the house was affectionately called "The Knoll."

Delta Chi

1913 brought three from the Pacific Coast and one from Texas.

The 1913 convention established a traveling secretary for uniform inspections of the chapters. This was an expensive proposition for the fraternity. It was essential to choose the right man for the job. The *Quarterly* editor urged, "When you have the right man for traveling inspector, do all you possibly can to keep him there…Do not make the mistake of changing inspectors each convention. Keep politics out of it all the time. Make the salary large enough for a large man; be practical. Here's to the success of our first traveling secretary; long may he inspect." George B. Bush (Stanford '10) accepted the position. He was an often seen presence at Delta Chi functions across the country. "Here's to George, we know that he will set a record of efficiency in this office that will not be equaled in many a long day." Bush encouraged brothers to think less of their chapters and more of Delta Chi as a whole.

The Toronto convention raised another issue that would contribute to the general fraternity debate. A proposal was submitted to make eligible for admission the sons and brothers of existing members, even though the men did not intend to study law. There was heated discussion before the proposal was voted down. A Chicago brother questioned, "Are we doing ourselves justice? Is it not compatible with the best interests of Delta Chi, to broaden our view whereby we shall permit the admission of brothers and sons, at least? It is so and right. It should be done. Let's make it a stronger family affair.

Let us not miss so much of the best material, now lost to the order." The May 1914 issue of the *Quarterly* reported that Delta Upsilon had forbidden membership of its members in Delta Chi. "It is a severe jolt to our self-esteem to find the earnest, if not informed, editor of the *Delta Upsilon Quarterly* of the opinion that Delta Upsilon should make careful note of the fact that members of that honorable non-secret society are not permitted to join Delta Chi. Allow us to reassure the D.U.s that it is unnecessary for them to take note, for no Delta Upsilon will ever be invited to join a chapter of Delta Chi. Nor will a member of any other general fraternity."

In 1915 the University of Pennsylvania put a policy into place that all universities would eventually adopt and which would greatly impact the nature of Delta Chi. The rule going into effect was that only holders of college degrees were allowed admission into the law school. The Pennsylvania Chapter wrote, "Our chapter was dealt quite a blow - just how hard remains to be seen - by a new rule going into effect in the fall of 1915…This means that we will have to concentrate on the college department harder than ever." In order to compete, chapters initiated men who intended to later study law giving Delta Chi even more of a general character. Cornell reported on their condition, "…the boys have plunged into the rushing season with Delta Chi vigor and when the foam has settled if determination means anything, the incoming class will stand in the shoes of those who have gone before." Pledge badges were $0.50 and the official fraternity badge price had been reduced by some heavy negotiating from $5.00 to $3.50. The 1915 convention declared Delta Chi jewelry could only be purchased through the national treasurer, who registered each item. Convention minutes noted the duty had been imposed upon

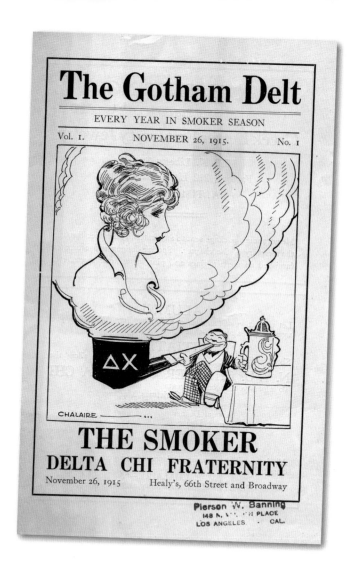

The Gotham Delt

EVERY YEAR IN SMOKER SEASON

Vol. I.   NOVEMBER 26, 1915.   No. I

CHALAIRE

THE SMOKER
DELTA CHI FRATERNITY
November 26, 1915   Healy's, 66th Street and Broadway

Pierson W. Banning
148 N. ... PLACE
LOS ANGELES - CAL.

the "DD" to supply the chapters and members with pins, pledge buttons, and keys. "The scheme will insure uniformity, guarantee quality, and save members some money."

The California Chapter reported in February 1914 that they had formed a Delta Chi orchestra. "Two cornets, a violin, clarinet, flute and piano constitute our 'material.' Rather unseemly for a body of law students, yet quite consistent with their noble purpose-to adjust inharmonious conditions, is the interest we invest in music." Cornell brothers were proud of their record in inter-fraternity bowling. "After getting off to a bad start, the boys recovered from their slump and won consistently from then on."

The Henry Ford Peace Ship

Three Delta Chis joined automobile magnate Henry Ford on a mission for peace in 1915. Ford had no patience for conventional diplomacy and was supremely frustrated by the war in Europe. He asked a reporter, "If I can make automobiles run, why can't I steer those people clear of war?" Confident in his ability to impact foreign leaders, Ford gathered a diverse delegation including thirty college students, three of whom were George Wythe (Texas '16), Walter Hixenbaugh Jr. (Nebraska '16), and C. A. Sorenson (Nebraska '13). Leaving the Hoboken, New Jersey docks on December 4, 1915, the group traveled aboard the *Oscar II* to neutral European capitals, espousing pacifism as they went. The Ford expedition was ridiculed by the press and denounced by the United States government. Brother Wythe reported to the *Quarterly*, "One of the most pleasant features of the trip over was the opportunity to know Mr. Ford. He would get out on deck without hat or coat, in the morning or just before retiring for the night, and race around with some of us fellows until we were out of breath. He seemed never to tire...Mr. Ford's departure at Christiania hurt the expedition very much, for his charming personality would have won over the people of the foreign countries just as it did the newspaper men on the *Oscar II*."

The delegation, minus Ford, crossed Germany via railroad. "We were only in the Kaiser's domains during twelve hours of darkness." Wythe described the German soldier in charge of their railcar, "He had a spiked helmet with eagles; also had an iron cross; also a shattered leg... he knocked on the door of our compartment and when I opened it to see what he wanted he said: 'Ta, ta, you are now in the country hated by all the world.'" The three Delta Chis returned to New York on the RMS *Noordam*. After a harrowing nineteen-day crossing from Rotterdam, the brothers landed in Hoboken on January 29, 1916. The ship's captain called the trip the worst in his thirty-two years at sea. Reflecting on the fact that Ford had chartered the ships and paid all the delegations' expenses, Wythe concluded, "...All were unanimous in declaring that Mr. Ford's was the finest house party they had ever attended." Many of the students would return from this hopeful mission of peace to begin training to go to war.

Delta Chi Brothers Wythe (Texas '16), Hixenbaugh (Nebraska '16), and Sorenson (Nebraska '13) were invited to join Henry Ford's peace delegation in 1915. *Library of Congress, Bain News Service*

Chapter houses began to report they had telephones. Southern California was delighted to have both hot and cold running water twenty-four hours a day. Brothers socialized both in the house and outside the house as a group. Michigan men were instructed on the rules of drinking before they were initiated. "They are told not to buy drinks for others unless it is for a visiting Delt; also not to drink anything stronger than beer downtown. Friday and Saturday nights they may drink more if under the supervision of upperclassmen."

As the fraternity celebrated its twenty-fifth anniversary in 1915 there were twenty-three active chapters. Since its organization an average of 298 men a year were initiated. As would be expected, the older chapters were disproportionally represented on the "XX". Cornell had provided six "AAs" and Chicago-Kent, four. Newer chapters, however, were beginning to make a showing.

While social events seemed to occupy the minds of many, Canadian Delta Chis had much more serious concerns to consider. When Great Britain declared war on Germany in August 1914, Canada, as a part of the British Empire, was automatically involved. Canadian men, including many Delta Chis, rushed to enlist. J. G. Bole (Osgoode Hall '15) wrote, "So we find ourselves at the beginning of a new existence. More surely than ever before do we realize ourselves an integral part of a great empire-an empire close-knit, confident, not unprepared. What the end will be no man dare say." W. F. Huycke ("E" of Osgoode Hall) wrote, "Osgoode is doing its little bit to help, and it would not be betraying any military secrets to mention the fact that Osgoode Hall has its rifle corps, and

California Delta Chis encouraged all to attend the San Francisco convention in 1915. "We have a saloon, also a church. There are more girls to the square inch here than we know what to do with."

Georgetown Chapter Halloween Dance, November 1915.

Convention delegates received a special plaque commemorating Delta Chi Day at the Panama Pacific International Exposition.

The 1915 convention coincided with the Panama Pacific International Exposition in San Francisco. *Edward H. Mitchell, San Francisco, California, 1911*

Delta Chis serving in the Seventy-fourth Battalion Canadian Expedition Force were listed in the August 1916 *Quarterly*.

356   DELTA CHI QUARTERLY

THE DELTA CHI ROLL OF HONOR.

74TH BATTALION CANADIAN EXPEDITION FORCE.

Headquarters Exhibition Barracks, Toronto, Canada, February 13, 1916.
To the Editor of the Delta Chi Quarterly:

Although our chapter has broken up for the time being, as many as could get together last night for the annual dance. As we ran over the list of our members away, I thought I would drop you a line and let you see how our ranks have been depleted.

You probably won't realize how this country is bound up in the present war. The result is that practically all the fraternity houses here are either closed or about to be closed. The best of our University men are going overseas as fast as they can.

Although you won't know many personally, I thought perhaps you might be interested in the Delta Chi roll of honor. It is as complete as I can get it. Some are over now. Ward Wright, Grover Kappele, Orr and myself will probably be over very soon. This is the list:

Lieut. Col. Hopkins, formerly 2nd Batt. Killed.

Capt. Greenlees, 7th Battery Canadian Field Artillery.

Captain Foster, 19th Battalion, Canadian Expeditionary Force. Wounded, now returned to France.

Lieut. Clive Thompson, 19th Batt. C. E. F.

Private Gordon Bole, M. G. S. 19th Batt. C. E. F.

Lieut. R. Hette, Royal Field Artillery.

Lieut. Marsh (Michigan Chapter) 15th Battery, C. F. A.

Major Walter Gow, 35th Batt. C. E. F.

Lieut. H. Saer, formerly 35th, now C. F. A.

Lieut. Kennedy, 37th Batt. C. E. F.

Private Norman Keys, Princess Patricia's Canadian Light Infantry.

Lieut. Sidney Wedd, Imperial Army.

Lieut. H. B. Daw, 58th Batt. C. E. F.

Lieut. W. F. Huycke, 39th Overseas Batt. C. E. F.

Lieut. D. Huycke (pledged) 33rd Battery C. F. A.

Lieut. H. V. Hearst, 74th Overseas Batt. C. E. F.

Lieut. E. R. Kappele, 75th Overseas Batt. C. E. F.

Major Ward Wright, 81st Overseas Batt C. E. F.

Capt. Jno. J. Grover, 81st Overseas. Batt. C. E. F.

Capt. G. M. Orr, 81st Overseas Batt. C. E. F.

Lieut. Smeath, 83rd Overseas Batt. C. E. F.

Lieut. Geo. Kappele, G. G. B. G. Deceased.

Lieut. W. P. McKay, 139th Overseas Battalion C. E. F.

Lieut. Geo. Grover, 180th Overseas Battalion C. E. F.

Lieut. W. J. Beaton, 182nd Overseas Battalion C. E. F.

Lieut. B. Mile, Signalling Seg. Corps of Engineers.

Lieut. C. S. McKee, attached to G. S. O. 2nd division.

Lieut.-Colonel John A. Cooper, 198th Ov. Bn. C. E. F.

These also are in training classes or about to be attached:

Lieut. F. Elliott, 9th Mississauga Horse. (Militia.)

Lieut. W. Wood.

Lieut. C. E. L. Babcock, 156th Ov. Bn. C. E. F.

Lieut. G. M. Willoughby, Artillery.

Lieut. Gorden Balfour, Artillery.

Lieut. E. M. Rowand, Artillery.

Lieut. H. W. Shoplen, 2nd Regt. Militia.

As you will see these 35 are a large percentage of our chapter active and alumni. Many of the graduates are not in a position to go, either from age or physical reasons and all interests are bent on the prosecution of the war.

I hope things in the Fraternity generally are prospering, and that when the war is over we may have a revival of the Osgoode Chapter with renewed life.

With best regards and best wishes,

Fraternally yours,

HOWARD V. HEARST.

(Editor's Note: Since the receipt of this letter we have learned that Brother Harold Foster has been mentioned in dispatches and Brothers Wedd and Keyes have been wounded.)

The Southern California Chapter mailed invitations to alumni asking for their presence at a 1916 initiation ceremony.

Minnesota Delta Chi planned a 1916 party at White Bear Lake.

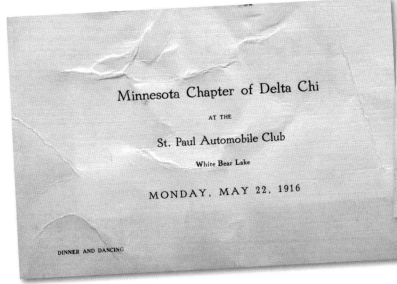

that Delta Chis are spending part of their time in learning to march and shoot."

American brothers made light passing references to the war. "Sam has passed the bar examination, but before settling down to the practice of law has started out to do some globe trotting… When the war clouds roll by and the veil of censorship lifts, we shall expect to hear of his adventures and feats on the battle-ground of Europe." The Los Angeles Alumni Chapter even gathered to play war. More than fifty Delta Chis divided into German and Ally camps. "The fight was fast and furious and the number of watermelons thrown into the camp of the enemy was appalling. The terrible havoc resulting from the bursting melons, the flying shell and many black seeds continued until from sheer

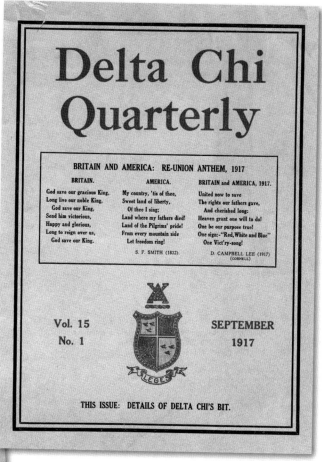

The tone of the *Quarterly* sobered dramatically after the United States declared war in 1917. The editor put up the battle cry, "Don't let the Kaiser kill Delta Chi."

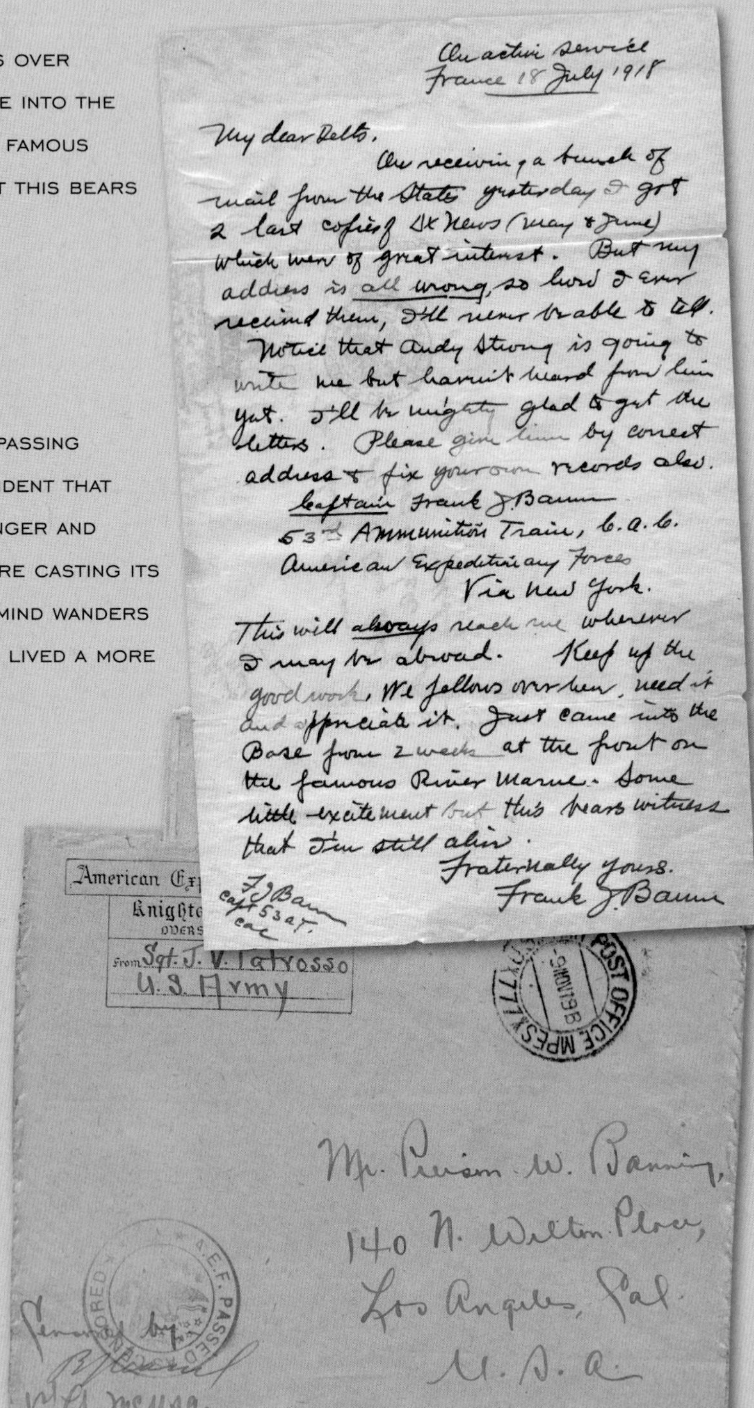

"ON ACTIVE SERVICE, FRANCE 18 JULY 1918

MY DEAR DELTS,

KEEP UP THE GOOD WORK. WE FELLOWS OVER
HERE NEED IT AND APPRECIATE IT. JUST CAME INTO THE
BASE FROM 2 WEEKS AT THE FRONT ON THE FAMOUS
RIVER MARNE. SOME LITTLE EXCITEMENT BUT THIS BEARS
WITNESS THAT I'M STILL ALIVE.

FRATERNALLY YOURS,

F.G.B"

"DEAR PIERSON,

IT IS VERY APPARENT THE DELTA CHI IS PASSING
THROUGH A GREAT CRISIS, BUT I FEEL CONFIDENT THAT
AFTER IT IS ALL OVER SHE WILL ARISE STRONGER AND
BETTER FOR THE EFFORT...WITH A BRIGHT FIRE CASTING ITS
CHEERFUL SHADOWS ABOUT THE ROOM, MY MIND WANDERS
BACK TO THE OLD ANTE-WAR DAYS WHEN ONE LIVED A MORE
CIVILIZED EXISTENCE AND DIDN'T CONSIDER
IT AS NECESSARY OR GOOD FORM TO BRAG
WHEN HE TOOK A BATH, THE NOW THE
CREAM OF LUXURIES... THE WAR SITUATION
HAS BEEN VERY ENCOURAGING OF LATE
AND WITH THE DOWNFALL OF BULGARIA,
TURKEY AND AUSTRIA, WE ALL FEEL THAT
THE UNCONDITIONAL SURRENDER OF
GERMANY IS BUT A QUESTION OF DAYS...
WELL, PIERSON, THE HOUR GROWS LATE
AND THE CANDLE—MY LAST—FLICKERS IN
ITS LAST FULL STRUGGLE FOR EXISTENCE,
SO MUST SAY AU REVOIR. REMEMBER ME
TO ALL OF THE OLD BUNCH, AND LET
ME HEAR FROM YOU WHEN OPPORTUNITY
AFFORDS. WITH BEST WISHES TO
YOURSELF I AM, AS EVER,

PAT [SGT. JULIUS V. PATROSSO,
SOUTHERN CALIFORNIA '12]

AMBULANCE CO. 162, AMERICAN EXPEDITIONARY FORCES"

exhaustion of the resources of each country, the war ended." The men would soon look longingly back on this time of innocent fun.

John B. Harshman ("DD") tried to prepare chapters for the financial impact of impending war. In 1917 letters to all chapter "Ds" he wrote, "Under war conditions each chapter will have its special problems, but all will meet the same high prices and more or less the same inroads by the war upon the chapter roll with corresponding reductions in chapter receipts. Thus this is going to be a year when greater vigilance, economy and efficiency must be exercised…" Harshman emphasized the need to "…push your 'clean-up' campaign to a speedy termination…The future of your chapter and even of the Fraternity will be deeply effected thereby." Conditions made it unthinkable to continue with the scheduled 1917 convention. Trying to provide continuity of leadership, members of the "XX" traveled to Neponsit, Long Island, at their own expense to meet at John Kuhn's seashore bungalow during the summer of 1917. The men, presuming they would soon be at war, all resigned their positions. Needing someone to fill the "AA" position, they looked to the forty-year-old

Kuhn who was without previous military training. In later memoirs Kuhn wrote, "…the probabilities were that I would not even pass the exacting physical examination then required for admission to the officers' training camp. Furthermore, that being beyond draft age, there was less chance that I'd be in the service than most of them. That's how I came to be drafted into accepting the mandate to be 'AA' the second time." Contrary to these predictions, Kuhn left the United States for France in May 1918 as a first lieutenant of field artillery. Delegates would not gather for the twentieth international convention until the conclusion of the war in 1919.

The 1919 Minneapolis convention focused on one looming question: Shall Delta Chi become a general fraternity? Two men clearly voiced the opposing sides of the issue. John J. Kuhn (Cornell '98, "AA" from 1906–07 and again during the crucial time of 1917–21) passionately advocated remaining a law fraternity. Assuming the role of editor of the *Quarterly* in 1916, Roger Steffan (Ohio State '13) frequently editorialized in strong support of the general membership movement. In the May 1929 *Quarterly* Steffan

Delta Chis at Camp Dix in 1917 included, seated, Lawrence H. Green (Georgetown '09), Walter G. Evans (Cornell '09), Cyrus S. Kauffman (Minnesota '17), Romaine Shephard (Union '12), George B. VanBuren (Cornell '16), and Howard R. Aldridge (NYU '08). Back row, John J. Kuhn (Cornell 1898) and Edward D. Bolton (NYU '08).

Roger Steffan (Ohio State '13), as editor of the *Quarterly,* was a loud voice in favor of the general membership movement.

Hands Across the Centuries

recalled the struggle of 1919. "I remember the night well. The magazine was practically ready to print and I was completing the editorials. Suddenly it struck like a dazzling light: 'Why Delta Chi's a humbug. We're posing before the world as a law fraternity and we haven't been a law fraternity for seven or eight years. True, a few chapters remain true to the law tradition but most of them are general.' And thereupon I decided to lift my piping voice in behalf of making Delta Chi an honest woman…" Billy Bride stood squarely between the opposing views and was determined to find a compromise. Bride wrote, "We have a serious issue before us and it will settle itself if we don't tear our hair and lose our tempers. We are all Delta Chi whatever may be our views on the question of our becoming a general fraternity. With a little give and take, the right side will win." Both sides put forth proposals at the 1919 convention with

neither proposal passing. The only amendment passed with no opposition was to allow brothers and sons of Delta Chis, regardless of their courses of study, to be eligible for membership. The Minneapolis convention ended with emotions running high, the question of general membership unresolved, and the future of the fraternity in jeopardy.

The pro-law Kuhn sent a letter to all chapters in October 1919. "After four days spent in earnest thought, wise debate and deliberation, the recent Minneapolis Convention definitely and conclusively settled the question, raised by some chapters, against Delta Chi changing into a general fraternity. This work may be unpopular with some…but a united effort to live up in good faith to the letter and spirit of our Constitution, which we are <u>all</u> sworn to obey, and which it is my duty to enforce, means that Delta Chi will continue in her glorious record in her thirtieth year, and continue to help those who are fortunate to be among her membership." Executive director since 1979, Raymond Galbreth describes Kuhn's letter as "a last ditch cheer." It was by no means the end of the debate. In November of that year, Cornell sent out a plea. Alumni were invited to the chapter house for a smoker on November 15. The dismal results of the rushing season were presented and the question asked, "What are we to do?" Alumni who opposed the general fraternity idea admitted the situation was grave yet offered no solution. The decade turned with the status of Delta Chi still hanging in the balance.

Daniel A. Reed (Cornell 1898) served in the House of Representatives from 1919 until his death in 1959. Reed, a former Cornell varsity football player, was the head football coach at Cincinnati, Penn State, and Cornell before serving in Congress.

Dead In Our Country's Service

This is a group of Delta Chis who died in action. Left to right, upper row: Lieut. H. B. Daw, Lieut. John C. Sandall, Lieut. Ralph Laughlin; center: Lieut. Richard Vaughn; lower row: Lieut. E. R. Churchill, Lieut. John Wiley Day, Corporal William H. Scott.

FOR THESE—GOLD STARS

Cornell
. Leslie Herbert Groser, '13, killed in action.

★ ★ ★ ★

Lieut. Walter Seely Jones, '13, killed in action
ptember 16, 1918.

★ ★ ★ ★

James Carter Knapp, '20, killed in action
vember 10, 1918.

★ ★ ★ ★

New York
H. Stevenson Whalen, '09, died at Ft. Hous-
July 26, 1916.

★ ★ ★ ★

Michigan
. Hatch, killed in action.

★ ★ ★ ★

Dickinson
Richard Vaughn, '20, killed in action, Sep-
8, 1918.

★ ★ ★ ★

ohn Wiley Day, '10, killed in action.

★ ★ ★ ★

Chicago-Kent
kins, '15, died at Camp Mills, October 10,

★ ★ ★ ★

Earl H. Linn, '17, died in camp.

★ ★ ★ ★

elville Stephens, '18, killed in training

★ ★ ★ ★

. Lyons, '13, died at Camp Grant, October,

★ ★ ★ ★

Buffalo
Rockwell Churchill, '16, killed in action,
7, 1918.

★ ★ ★ ★

illiam H. Scott, '18, killed in action.

★ ★ ★ ★

Osgoode Hall
es Hopkins, '08, killed in accident.

★ ★ ★ ★

r MacMurrich, '98, killed in action.

★ ★ ★ ★

Col. John McDonald Mowat, '98, killed in action
October 8, 1916.

★ ★ ★ ★

Hubert Patterson Osborne, '15, killed in action
July 7, 1917.

★ ★ ★ ★

Lieut. James Gordon Bole, killed in action.

★ ★ ★ ★

Lieut. Ernest Reece Kappele, killed at Vimy Ridge.

Union
Romaine Shepard, '12, killed in action.

★ ★ ★ ★

Ohio State
1st Lieut. Ralph W. Laughlin, killed in action, September 20, 1918.

★ ★ ★ ★

Chicago
Lieut. John Chester Sandall, killed in action.

★ ★ ★ ★

Georgetown
Lieut. William Sheehan, '11, killed in action, September, 1918.

★ ★ ★ ★

Harold Breen Hall, '18, died at Camp Upton, September, 1918.

★ ★ ★ ★

Vaughn E. Smith, '16, killed in action.

★ ★ ★ ★

Capt. John Douglas Wade, '06, killed in action.

★ ★ ★ ★

Walter B. Sadler, '15, killed in action.

★ ★ ★ ★

Pennsylvania
Capt. Paris Carlisle, '15, killed in action.

★ ★ ★ ★

Lieut. William H. Mulvihill, '16, killed in aero fall,
Arcadia, Fla.

★ ★ ★ ★

Earlston D. Hargett, '17, killed in action.

★ ★ ★ ★

Howard Baker, '12, died at Camp Sherman.

★ ★ ★ ★

Virginia
W. P. Doson, '14, killed in action.

★ ★ ★ ★

Wyatt Rushton, '13, died in service.

★ ★ ★ ★

W. S. Powell, '18, died in service.

★ ★ ★ ★

Texas
1st Lieut. Robert Skiles, died of influenza.

★ ★ ★ ★

Nebraska
Lieut. Richard Cook, killed in action.

★ ★ ★ ★

Southern California
Sergt. Dean B. Nethaway, '16, died at Camp Logan,
October 1, 1918.

★ ★ ★ ★

Walter F. Trask, died at Rochester, Minn., January
20, 1919.

★ ★ ★ ★

California
Dee Truit, died at U. S. Military Academy.

Returning from the trenches, Delta Chis left behind were not forgotten.

> *"The ideals we strove for in the War did not bring the millennium we hoped. We must not be discouraged, but with more earnest endeavor live to make Delta Chi a real influence in the world."*
>
> HOWARD V. HEARST (OSGOODE HALL '13)

Chapter newspapers flourished in the 1920s.

In the year following the Minneapolis convention, thirteen of twenty-one existing chapters admittedly initiated or pledged men who were not eligible under strict interpretation of the constitution. Even within the eight active chapters who stayed true to the constitution, there were men majoring in engineering, commerce, the arts, and agriculture admitted under the brother and son eligibility provision. Despite great expansion in the popularity of fraternities, it had been six years since the baby Delta Chi chapter, Kentucky, had been installed. Ignoring the controversy, active chapters plunged head first into the Roaring Twenties. Most chapters had veterans returning from service who were considerably older than the average college student. These older men brought mature leadership to the chapters and were treated with great respect.

An effort was made to compile a record of all Delta Chis serving in World War I. "Whether your service took you 'over the top' in Flanders or whether your service was 'over the top' of a desk in Washington, you were helping with the great battle for civilization and we want to know what you did." Eighteen men from the Osgoode Chapter alone gave the supreme sacrifice. All the active members of the chapter had enlisted en masse in 1914. Nearly one hundred Osgoode Hall members saw active service during the war. The Osgoode brothers lost spanned the entire history of the chapter, including a charter member and the last initiate before the outbreak of war. E. H. Saer (Osgoode "C" 1918) reported on the chapter's condition at war's end. "Returning to civil life in the fall of 1918, I found only 4 members of the active chapter of the fraternity left and they were all in their final year, which meant that from April 1919 on, we would be without active membership." Initiating four pledges in January of 1919, Saer went on to report, "These four initiates form now the nucleus upon which we hope to build up again a strong chapter."

"AA" John J. Kuhn continued to vehemently argue to maintain the fraternity's law nature. In a rather grandiose declaration Kuhn wrote, "I am in touch with conditions, and ought to know." As *Quarterly* editor, Roger Steffan (Ohio State '13) continued to attack Kuhn with full force in his editorials, "The real trouble with the 'AA' however is not that he doesn't know, but that he can't read. Of course if he won't read the chapter letters in the *Quarterly*...telling him that these chapters have initiated non-law men. No one can make him read. One can't take him to the kindergarten again and show him how to put the letters together. If he prefers to believe that 'e-n-g-i-n-e-e-r' spells 'lawyer' and 'j-o-u-r-n-a-l-i-s-t' spells 'pre-law' why that is the privilege of any free American but it is not good spelling." Heated correspondence flew like the letter to Founder Frederick Whitney written by Herman J. Westwood (Cornell '94) passionately arguing against change. "I know this is a long letter, but the great, live thing which you helped to found is in danger and to save it worth my

Parley Parks Christensen (Cornell '97) was the presidential nominee of the Farmer-Labor Party in 1920.

A CONTRIBUTION BY "AA" KUHN

FOR EXCHANGE: Fraternity, over thirty years old, offers to irrevocably exchange its legal traditions and character and its reputation of maintaining an intellectual ideal in college life, for a mere spirit of general fraternity good-fellowship. Its original ideals were recently approved by the Inter-Fraternity Conference, composed of all the leading Greek Letter Fraternities, and are sure to be soon in much demand.

Here is an opportunity to obtain solid gold for new shiny nickle plate. Apply immediately, as this offer is likely to be soon withdrawn, in view of determined internal opposition.

ALLADIN.

The Virginia Chapter men posed in 1921. Back row center, wearing a bow tie, is Peyton Rhodes. He later became president of Southwestern College in Memphis, Tennessee, which was renamed Rhodes College in his honor.

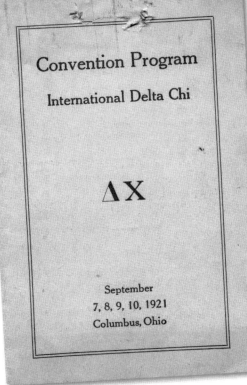

Convention Program

International Delta Chi

ΔX

September
7, 8, 9, 10, 1921
Columbus, Ohio

INTERNATIONAL CONVENTION

Delta Chi

COLUMBUS, OHIO, SEPT. 7-8-9-10

Banquet—Deshler Hotel

Coupon No. 5   5

Supper—Scioto Country Club
Coupon No. 4

Luncheon—Elks' Club
Coupon No. 3

Corn Roast
Coupon No. 2

7:00 P. M. BANQUET, BALL ROOM DESH-
LER HOTEL. Coupon No. 5.

effort to write the letter and yours to read it." Founders Albert S. Barnes and Peter S. Johnson joined the cry to accept progress over tradition and allow Delta Chi to adapt to the changing times. Johnson wrote, "Right now we seem to need re-founding."

The first new chapter since 1913 was added in January of 1921. Wisconsin became the twenty-second name on the Delta Chi charter list. In an effort to continue expanding membership the Columbus, Ohio, convention in 1921 increased the categories of qualified members. As defined in a successful motion by Harry Wadsworth (Stanford '20), eligible members were white males pursuing studies in law, liberal arts, journalism, commerce, or finance. Also eligible were prospective law students and sons and brothers of Delta Chi members. It was maintained, however, that 25 percent of every chapter membership must be law, or pre-law, students. It quickly became clear that chapter compliance was going to be difficult, if not impossible. The 1921 convention also officially made October 13 Founders' Day. A constitutional amendment required, "On this date it shall be compulsory upon each chapter to hold a meeting, at which there shall be appropriate ceremonies, and at which a history of the Fraternity, prepared by the 'XX', shall be read."

Administration of the new eligibility requirements led to a realization

The March 1921 *Quarterly* featured some of Delta Chi's varsity athletes.

"CC" from 1906 until 1923, William W. "Billy" Bride (Georgetown '04) didn't let the chapters fall behind in their paperwork.

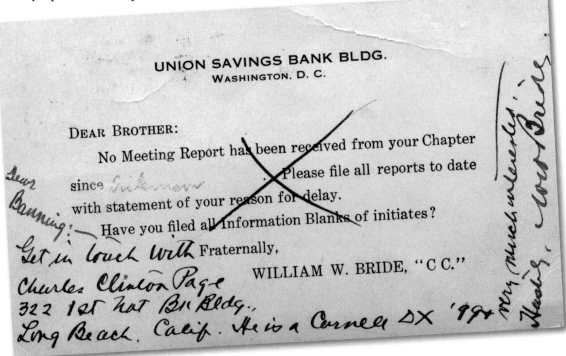

HANDS ACROSS THE CENTURIES

The cover of the September 1922 *Quarterly* trumpeted an end to the general fraternity debate.

that Delta Chi needed a central office and a full-time paid employee to manage this office and its affairs. While the "XX" considered the needs of the thirty-year-old fraternity, daily life at the chapter houses continued fairly smoothly. Chicago's steward, who ran a tailoring, pressing, and shoeshine shop in the basement for the boys, complained that late night revelers were stealing milk and pie from the kitchen. Ohio adopted the motto of "Etiquette Always" and firmly held to their policy that the name of a girl was never to be mentioned during meals. Union brothers adjusted to life without a maid and inaugurated a simple rule "by which each man was required to see that his room was cleaned and kept in presentable condition." Nebraska joyfully reported on the location of their new chapter house. "As soon as we purchased our new home, sororities seemed to flock to the scene. We are now completely surrounded by five of them and hardly know how to conduct ourselves."

Assuming the position of "AA" in 1921, Henry V. McGurren (Chicago-Kent '10) recognized the unworkable conditions created by the complex compromise of the Wadsworth amendment. He called a special meeting of the "XX" on April 29, 1922, at the La Salle Hotel in Chicago. His telegram to "XX" members read, "Most important business involving future welfare of fraternity. Your presence is most urgent. Wire whether you will be present." He explained, "I am convinced that it not only is desirable at this time to adopt the general fraternity amendment without delay, but that it is absolutely necessary for the unity and welfare of Delta Chi." The "XX" adopted a general fraternity constitutional amendment at this meeting, removing all remaining membership restrictions, and submitted it to the chapters for ratification. From the active chapters the only negative votes came from Buffalo, Dickinson,

Cornell announced with pride the completion of their new house in 1915.

STRUGGLES OVER THE STATUS OF THE CORNELL CHAPTER HOUSE REFLECTED THE EMOTIONAL DEBATE OVER GENERAL FRATERNITY STATUS. BUILT BY THE GENEROUS CONTRIBUTIONS OF CORNELL ALUMNI AND COMPLETED IN 1915, HOME TO THE MOTHER CHAPTER WAS CALLED "THE KNOLL." CONTROL OF THE HOUSE RESTED LARGELY WITH THE DELTA CHI REALTY COMPANY BOARD OF DIRECTORS, COMPOSED OF CORNELL ALUMNI. WAR CONDITIONS, COMBINED WITH MEMBERSHIP DIFFICULTIES PRIOR TO ADOPTING GENERAL FRATERNITY STATUS, LED THE HOUSE TO ACCUMULATE CONSIDERABLE DEBT. THE ENTIRE DELTA CHI REALTY COMPANY BOARD OPPOSED THE GENERAL FRATERNITY MOVEMENT. IF THIS BECAME THE FRATERNITY POLICY, THEY REFUSED TO RAISE FUNDS FOR THE CORNELL CHAPTER HOUSE. THE FRATERNITY, IN TURN, REFUSED TO ACCEPT THE DICTATES OF ONE SMALL GROUP.

ROGER STEFFAN (OHIO STATE '13), THEN EDITOR OF THE *QUARTERLY*, PLEADED AGAINST THE PLAN IN A LETTER TO THE GROUP'S LEADER, WINTHROP TAYLOR (CORNELL '07). TAYLOR'S REPLY WAS BITTER. "UPON MY RETURN FROM A VACATION I FIND YOUR LETTERS... WITH REFERENCE TO WHAT YOU CHARACTERIZE 'THE LOSS OF CORNELL'S CHAPTER HOUSE.' I AM NOT AWARE OF ANY PLAN, WHICH HAS FOR ITS OBJECT THE DISCONTINUANCE OF THE USE OF THE PROPERTY AT ITHACA FOR HOUSING A GROUP OF LAW STUDENTS, PURSUANT TO THE AVOWED PURPOSES AND SPIRIT OF THE CONSTITUTION, LAWS AND TRADITIONS OF THE DELTA CHI FRATERNITY. I AM AWARE OF A PLAN, OF WHICH I APPROVE, WHICH HAS THIS VERY PURPOSE IN VIEW."

THE DELTA CHI REALTY COMPANY PLAYED THEIR HAND BY TRANSFERRING OWNERSHIP OF THE HOUSE TO CORNELL UNIVERSITY TO BE USED AS HOUSING FOR HONOR STUDENTS. THE INDIVIDUAL ALUMNI INVOLVED BENEFITTED FROM THE TRANSFER BY RECEIVING CREDIT AS CONTRIBUTORS TO THE UNIVERSITY. AFTER TITLE WAS PASSED, THE UNIVERSITY REALIZED THE UNDERLYING PLAN WAS FAULTY AT BEST. CORNELL THEN OFFERED TO SELL THE HOUSE BACK TO THE DELTA CHI REALTY COMPANY. TO ASSIST IN MAKING THIS POSSIBLE, THE GENERAL FRATERNITY MADE A LOAN TO THE REALTY COMPANY. AND THUS, ONCE AGAIN THE CORNELL HOUSE RETURNED TO DELTA CHI'S OWNERSHIP.

In June 1921, the Delta Chi Realty Company offered the house as a gift to Cornell University in protest of the general fraternity movement.

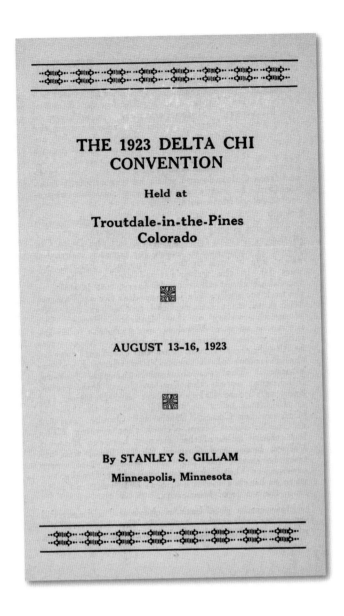

THE 1923 DELTA CHI CONVENTION

Held at

Troutdale-in-the-Pines Colorado

AUGUST 13-16, 1923

By STANLEY S. GILLAM
Minneapolis, Minnesota

The 1925 Iowa golf team included Brothers Williams, Dickenson, Allen, and Whitehead.

and Osgoode Hall. No chapters were lost in the transition but some chose to remain only law chapters. The general fraternity amendment was formally adopted on June 6, 1922. In recounting the news the *Quarterly* editor wrote, "It became such a universal topic of debate that nearly everyone was sick and tired of it." The discussion, ongoing since 1909, could finally be left behind.

Delta Chis reflected the world around them in both large and small ways. Iowa reported, "The epidemic of corduroy trousers which has been sweeping over the campus here has at last found lodging in the Delta Chi House. Starting at first among the freshmen it has increased until the peculiar sound caused by a man walking about with these trousers on is a common thing around the chapter house."

The delegates to the 1923 convention in Troutdale, Colorado, appeared to stay true to the edicts of Prohibition. "Any who remember the conventions of any fraternity of ten, fifteen and twenty years ago, will recall a flowing spigot and a mammoth stein as the central figures of the picture. If anyone saw a drink of liquor at Troutdale he was a better sleuth than the writer of these homely topics. From the time the special train left Chicago to the time the last groups said farewell at Denver after visiting Estes Park, it was the soberest, hardest working convention we ever saw."

At this convention the necessary central office, complete with a managing director, and the national leadership were streamlined. The fifteen-member governing board had grown unwieldy, so the group was reduced to seven members. The "XX", composed of the "AA", "CC", "DD", "EE", and three members at large, acted as the governing body between conventions. To increase the chapters' representation, each elected one "BB" to the "XX". The "BB" acted as an alumni advisor and represented his chapter and acted as its spokesman. The most important functions of the "BB" were to oversee pledge training and monitor completion of the chapter objectives. The 1923 convention officially codified the fraternity's policy of expansion. "The Delta Chi Fraternity believes in expansion in educational institutions of recognized standing and regards with special favor state endowed institutions, where the petitioning body is of sufficient strength to meet the high ideals of our fraternity." This policy was reconfirmed, as written, at the 1925 and 1927 conventions. Although most delegates seemed to enjoy gathering at conventions there were always a few who grumbled. John C. Grover wrote to Odis

Executive director from 1929 to 1951, O. K. Patton (Iowa '12), center, visited with Brothers Huber (Chicago-Kent '26) and Higgins (Syracuse '12) at the 1925 convention.

Brothers Henry V. McGurren ("AA" 1913–17, 1921–27), William W. Bride ("AA" 1927–29), and John B. Harshman ("AA" 1929–35) traveled to Florida in 1926 for the thirtieth chapter's installation. These three men led the fraternity during many of its most pivotal years.

Delegates to the last convention of the 1920s paused for a moment during one of their banquets.

The Delta Chi
Mothers'
Club

Organized May 25, 1928

S. M. U. CHAPTER
1943-1944
Dallas, Texas

DELTA CHI
MOTHERS CLUB
Organized May 25
S. M. U.
1949
DALL

DELTA CHI
MOTHERS CLUB

*The
Delta C
1928-1929*

Mrs. Walter C. Connally.

Knight Patton after the 1927 convention, "All conventions are more or less a nightmare."

One Delta Chi was legendary on the Cornell campus. Addison Gifford Crowley was initiated in 1917 but did not graduate until 1938. Shortly after his initiation the entire Cornell Chapter joined the military service. While Crowley was serving as an officer in India, his father died leaving a trust for him with very specific

A Delta Chi Mother's Club was formed in 1927 at Texas and in 1928 at SMU. The clubs were active until the 1950s. Mrs. Walter C. Connally, mother of Fred H. Connally (Texas '25), was a founder and chairman of the Texas club. *Donated to the Delta Chi Archives by Fred H. Connally Jr.*

The December 1927 *Quarterly*, printed between editors, was only four pages long.

Sidney F. Taliaferro (Georgetown '13) was appointed by President Coolidge to serve as commissioner of the District of Columbia in 1927. Billy Bride wrote, "The chimes of Washington are pealing for 'Sid' Taliaferro, one of the best beloved men in Delta Chi." *Library of Congress, Harris & Ewing Collection*

instructions. Until the age of forty, as long as Crowley was attending college he would receive $300 a month. After returning from war, he found no appealing employment and decided to return to Cornell. He got his monthly check while studying a variety of subjects including law, architecture, and agriculture. A Cornell brother from the late 1920s, John C. Trussell ('28) vividly remembered Crowley living as an active in the chapter house. "He was a handsome and interesting chap, partially grey haired, smoked a pipe and wore tweed jackets. He was a stabilizing factor in the house during the depression years." At the age of forty Crowley inherited the bulk of the trust. He graduated in 1938 with a bachelor of landscape architecture. Finally leaving the Delta Chi house, he bought a bank in western New York and happily made himself president.

The central office, officially established by the 1923 convention, became more of a necessity after Delta Chi became a general fraternity. By the end of the decade the fraternity had blossomed to thirty-six chapters and the paperwork was overwhelming. Membership records had historically been located wherever the "CC" could be found. Charles H. Moore (NYU '00) recalled his term of "CC" beginning in 1901. "The official records which Westwood shipped to me upon my return to New York disclosed themselves as the contents of three old yellow box letter files." In the late 1920s, the "CC" was O. K. Patton, highly respected professor of law at the University of Iowa. Upon his election to the position in 1923 Patton stored the records in one room of a downtown Iowa City office building and hired a part-time secretary to handle Delta Chi affairs. As the fraternity expanded so did the records and the office was soon moved to 16½ South Clinton Street, a building owned by Patton. Patton was made executive secretary to the executive board following the 1929 convention. His one room devoted to Delta Chi became four rooms with four secretaries by 1929. This essentially established the international headquarters in Iowa City, where it remains today.

As with all organizations, politics were inevitably played in the selection of fraternity officers. A series of letters in April 1929 between O. K. Patton and John C. Grover confirm the discussions behind the scenes. Grover wrote, "I have been thinking over the question of 'AA' at the next convention – Gerstenberg, Marvin, Thompson and others. The objection that could be made to most of them is that they have not served the fraternity a sufficient time to justify this high honor…there is no man in the fraternity who fills these requirements better than John Harshman…write me what you think of it…" Patton replied, "John Harshman would be entirely satisfactory to me as a candidate. Indeed, Henry McGurren and I approached him on the matter at Thanksgiving time and it was then that I learned that he was pledged to support Milton Cornelius." Discussions must have continued for Harshman was the "AA" named at the 1929 convention. He led Delta Chi into the next decade and was in the office until 1935.

O. K. Patton visited with Dr. Cloyd H. Marvin (Stanford '15), president of the University of Arizona, and Charles W. Gerstenberg (NYU '04), 1930 chairman of the National Interfraternity Conference, at the 1927 convention held at Bigwin Inn at the Lake of Bays in Ontario (pictured left to right).

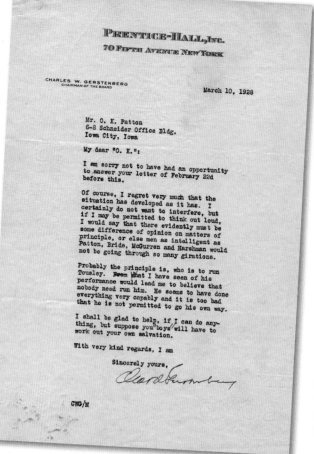

Charles W. Gerstenberg, one of the founders of the educational publishing company Prentice Hall, weighed in on heated internal discussions in 1928.

In May 1929, the Wisconsin Chapter posed on the lawn of their house at 142 East Gilman Street in Madison.

The 1929 convention delegates gathered in Estes Park, Colorado.

Chapter Five:
1930–1939

Shirley Temple, deemed Delta Chi Sweetheart by Dean C. M. Thompson during his term as "AA", sent the fraternity this picture in 1938. Thompson met the young actress in the late 1930s when visiting the Stanford Chapter where her brother, John S. "Jack" Temple, was a member. She wrote Thompson, "It would make me very proud and happy to be the Sweetheart of Delta Chi, and may I thank you for the honor in asking me."

Brother Grover "Ox" Emerson ('30), captain-elect of the Texas football team in 1931, showed Longhorn pledges a paddle on which was engraved ANTIQUE. This illustrated Delta Chi's commitment to its 1929 banishment of Hell Week.

"Forty years! To the undergraduate, what an age. To our founders, and hundreds of alumni, how quickly it has passed. To Delta Chi, destined to flourish as long as the Greek-letter system endures, just a fraction of its ultimate span."

JOHN B. HARSHMAN (OHIO STATE '07, "AA" 1929–35)

The 1930s began with the passing of Founder Myron McKee Crandall. He was the third Founder to die, Thomas D. Watkins and Thomas A. J. Sullivan preceding him. The *Quarterly* noted seven Founders remained with eight thousand sons to carry the fraternity forward. The Alumni Finance Control Board Plan, established in 1929, had become the budget-adopting and financial administrator of each chapter. The control board process was explained to the chapters by the field services supervisor, Ralph E. Prusok. "The first step in the procedure is to find four alumni who will devote some time to the chapter…If the alumni enforce the rules and by-laws under which the Control Board operates, the financial condition of any chapter may improve miraculously." Coordinating with the central office, the alumni boards prepared and submitted monthly operating statements from each chapter's books.

Scholarship became an area of great focus. With its scholarship program conceived in 1927 by O. K. Patton, Delta Chi was a leader in the fraternity world. Director of Scholarship Dr. Marsh W. White (Penn State faculty) continued the push toward academic excellence with a tutorial advisory system. George W. Obear (DePauw '30) reported, "I believe it safe to say that the tutorial advisers have already made some valuable contributions." The 1931 convention authorized annual awards of two trophies, one for the chapter ranking highest among all Delta Chi chapters scholastically and the other for the chapter making the greatest advance over its preceding year's record. For the 1930–31 school year, the first award was presented to the DePauw Chapter. The second award was given to the Alabama Chapter. In 1932 Marsh White reported the Delta Chi scholarship average topped that of the all-men average for the first time.

The Nebraska Chapter in the 1930s, at 1421 H Street, was positioned next door to the governor's mansion in Lincoln. The Nebraska boys routinely told tales of rubbing elbows with politics. As Nebraska governor from 1931 to 1935, Charles W. Bryan was well familiar with Delta Chi. His brother, William Jennings Bryan, was a proud and supportive member. Governor Bryan's relationship with the Delta Chis began when his first lady was locked out of the governor's mansion. Venturing next door for help, Mrs. Bryan spent an entire evening at the chapter house. "The ice was broken, and soon after, someone from the house borrowed the executive lawn mower for our own lawn.

Delta Chi Stands for . . .

SCHOLARSHIP

ALL HAIL . . . DEPAUW AND ALABAMA

Winners of our fraternity scholarship awards for the 1931-1932 School Year

DePauw and Alabama's academic achievements were evidence that the fraternity's focus on scholarship was working.

University of Illinois Economics Professor Frank G. Dickinson devised a mathematical formula, the Dickinson System, to determine the college football national champion from 1926 to 1940. He himself was the proud golf champion of the 1931 convention.

Federal Judge James H. Wilkerson (DePauw '92) put Al Capone behind bars in 1931 with a sentence of eleven years.

Louis A. Johnson (Virginia '12) helped found the American Legion and was national commander in 1932. He later served in the cabinet of President Harry S. Truman as the country's second secretary of defense.

Affably, the Bryans accepted a dinner invitation and came strolling over, like any congenial next door neighbors." Governor and Mrs. Bryan chaperoned the first Nebraska house dance of 1932 hosting a breakfast at the executive mansion the following morning.

Discussions of the Great Depression were prevalent but chapter activities continued. The Florida Chapter quipped, "Now we have no banks; consequently we can't lose any money!" *Quarterly* Editor Albert S. Tousley (Minnesota '24) mused, "From all that we've heard from our several chapters this past year, ping pong is going to supplant basketball, poker and petting, whichever one it is that is considered America's greatest indoor sport. Oh well, there are lots of things worse, and more expensive, than ping pong." The ping-pong craze filled the pages of the *Quarterly*. One headline read, "Ping-Pong Manly at Southern California," and another declared "Ping-Pong in Full Blast at Osgoode Hall." Regardless of these lighthearted articles, college students were not insulated from the Great Depression's impacts. The 1931–32 school year was the hardest year for Delta Chi since the war. Many chapters had depleted freshmen classes and lost seniors in record numbers.

Chapters were urged to consider the condition of the country's economy when planning their events. Few fraternities could afford the lavish parties of the Roaring Twenties. Even if parties could be thrown, the *Quarterly* issued a warning. "Those out of work resent bitterly the show of wealth displayed in some parts of our land, and many a hungry family might be fed for weeks with the money devoted to even one modest fraternity party. It may well be the 'smart' thing for fraternities to this year give part of their money allotted for entertainment to some organization caring for poor and unfortunate fellow citizens. Let Delta Chi set the example." Many chapters responded to this challenge. Radios were used for dances instead of orchestras, Osgoode Hall sold its cherished iceboat, and fines were imposed for leaving on lights or opening windows in the winter. Union invited local men in for meals and some brothers did their own butchering and dishwashing. Scheduled for August of 1933, the biennial convention was cancelled by the executive board. The active and alumni chapters voted unanimously in favor of the cancellation. "There is a limit to one's capacity, and perhaps a convention in 1933 would tax our young men beyond their limit."

Albert S. Tousley (Minnesota '24) shunned the unemployment lines and instead sought to accomplish a feat not successfully accomplished since 1881. In a seventeen-foot canoe he navigated all 2,530 miles of the Mississippi River. Tousley set out on Decoration Day, the last Monday of May 1932, from Lake Itasca, Minnesota. He bobbed in the Gulf of Mexico on September 15, more than three arduous months later.

As Tousley crossed into the Gulf of Mexico, another Delta Chi was racing toward Olympic gold. The 1932 Summer Olympic Games were held in Los Angeles despite the worldwide Great Depression. Brother Ivan Fuqua (Indiana '33) ran the opening leg of the 4x400 meter race for the American relay team. A track and field star at Indiana University, Fuqua was the university's first gold medal winner. The American runners set a new world record of 3:08.2 during the tenth Olympiad.

In 1934 conditions for the country at large, and the fraternity in general, were looking up. The thirty-seven chapters of Delta Chi pledged 485 men during the fall rushing season with an additional eighty-two men that winter. As

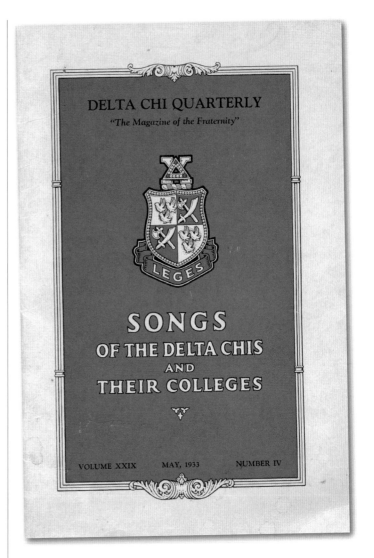

The third edition of the Delta Chi songbook was published in May of 1933. The price of the book was $0.50.

the fraternity ranks grew, members of the old guard continued to pass. Founder Owen Lincoln Potter who served as the first "AA" died in 1934.

UCLA and Michigan State were installed in 1935. Discussions were heated as to where the first convention since 1931 should be held. Eventually, Yellowstone National Park was chosen. The alumni dues program, established in 1935 at the Yellowstone convention, would play a large factor in carrying the fraternity through another difficult time on the horizon, World War II. A fixed amount of $5.00 was established as the amount of annual dues required of alumni not lifetime subscribers to

Ivan Fuqua (Indiana '35) was a gold medal winner in the 1932 Olympics and an All-American track star.

the *Quarterly*. Lifetime subscribers were required to pay $3.00. Payment of the annual dues gave alumni the latest edition of the fraternity directory, a membership card, a subscription to the *Quarterly*, and "the satisfaction of knowing you are helping the Fraternity carry on its ever widening program of activities in the realization of the ideal of the founders…"

An impressive number of Delta Chis competed in the controversial 1936 Olympics held in Berlin. Following in the footsteps of their brother Ivan Fuqua, two Indiana track stars traveled to Germany as well as the Indiana wrestling coach. Tommy Deckard and Don Lash were the Delta Chi Olympic runners. In

The 1935 Yellowstone convention was a productive gathering.

June of 1936 Lash broke the two-mile world record when he ran the distance in 8:59.6. He broke the existing record, set in 1931 by Paavo Nurmi, by a full 1.2 seconds. *Time* magazine reported on Lash's run describing it as "the best race-all things considered-ever run." In the Olympics, both Deckard and Lash participated in the men's 5,000-meter event with Lash placing thirteenth. William H. "Billy" Thom (Iowa '23) was appointed as head coach for the United States Olympic wrestling team. This honor resulted from a long career of successful coaching at Indiana. Ralph Bishop (Washington '36) was a member of the gold medal winning US Olympic basketball team, as was Frank Lubin (UCLA '31). Lubin, the child of Lithuanian immigrants, was later invited to go to Lithuania as the first coach of the country's national team and became known as the "Grandfather of Lithuanian basketball."

As Delta Chi branched beyond legal education, its graduating brothers pursued a wide variety of interesting occupations. P. Schuyler Miller

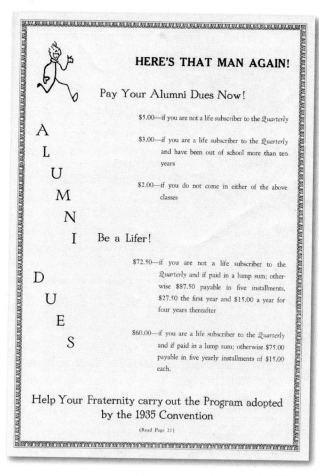

HERE'S THAT MAN AGAIN!

Pay Your Alumni Dues Now!

ALUMNI DUES

$5.00—if you are not a life subscriber to the *Quarterly*

$3.00—if you are a life subscriber to the *Quarterly* and have been out of school more than ten years

$2.00—if you do not come in either of the above classes

Be a Lifer!

$72.50—if you are not a life subscriber to the *Quarterly* and if paid in a lump sum; otherwise $87.50 payable in five installments, $27.50 the first year and $15.00 a year for four years thereafter

$60.00—if you are a life subscriber to the *Quarterly* and if paid in a lump sum; otherwise $75.00 payable in five yearly installments of $15.00 each.

Help Your Fraternity carry out the Program adopted by the 1935 Convention

(Read Page 21)

The alumni dues program would carry the fraternity through the difficult financial times of World War II.

John B. Harshman (Ohio State '07, "DD" 1913–29) enjoyed the Yellowstone convention on back of a donkey while O. K. Patton (Iowa '12) boarded a stagecoach.

Dr. Marsh White (Penn State faculty '20, "AA" 1952–54, "AA" emeritus, Order of the White Carnation), known for loudly leading Delta Chis in the song "Sweet Violets," was given a spray of the poseys to wear for the 1935 convention photo.

DELTA CHI QUARTERLY

In Memory of
William W. Bride
1881-1935

MAY, 1935

VOLUME XXXI   NUMBER 4

Sixteen pages of the May 1935 *Quarterly* honored William W. "Billy" Bride (Georgetown '04), former "CC", "EE", and "AA". "He shall live so long as Delta Chi shall endure. It is a monument to his achievement. It will never forget him."

(Union '31) was an amateur archeologist and writer who gained a cult following in the science fiction genre. Some of his pulp science fiction titles included *Alice in Blunderland*, *Trouble on Tantalus*, and *Fricassee in Four Dimensions*. His novel *Genus Homo*, published in 1941, is believed to be the earliest work of fiction dealing with the theme of intelligent apes usurping humanity. Another brother, Henry A. "Guy" Geidel (NYU '18), chose tennis as his profession after his service in World War I. He held the position of head pro at the Nassau Country Club at Glen Cove, New York, for thirteen years and was elected president of the Professional Lawn Tennis Association of the United States in 1936. Espy Hall (USC) made a name for himself in the West Coast speedboat racing circuit of the 1930s, winning the Class C hydroplane amateur title in 1934.

In an effort to protect the assets of each chapter, alumni finance control boards were promoted as the decade drew to a close. Authorized by the national governing board, local control boards consisted of four alumni and the "A" of a chapter. Their regular scrutiny and administration of chapter finances involved alumni in a concrete way, insured a realistic budget, and prevented individual members from graduating in debt to the chapter. The *Quarterly* espoused, "A working Alumni Control Board for every chapter by the 1938 Convention!" As the fraternity grew it became increasingly difficult for chapters to stay connected. "Buc" Buchanan and R. Mason "Macy" Blair reported regularly on their adventures as field secretaries. Established by the 1935 Yellowstone convention, the position of field secretary was generally given to young brothers just out of college and was not intended to be a long-term occupation. It was believed that "one with the undergraduate viewpoint can educate actives and pledges on national purposes and policies better than an older person."

Fathers and Sons, Now Brothers

William W. Bride Sr. and William W. Bride Jr. posed at the 1929 Estes Park convention. Bride Sr. was serving as "AA" at the time and Bride Jr. was a new initiate.

A generation of sons began to enter Delta Chi as brothers. The sons of three former "AAs"—Henry V. McGurren (Chicago-Kent '10), Edward W. Wright (Osgoode Hall '08), and William W. Bride (Georgetown '04)—were pledged in the 1930s. Carrying on their fathers' tradition of fraternity service, the sons of Wright and McGurren both became "As" of their respective chapters. A 1930s *Quarterly* noted, "There is something inspiring about the continuity that is thus established, and we hope that in the years to come the sons of other members, whether they have been officers or merely loyal members in the ranks, will accept membership in the same fraternity and wear the same pin that has meant so much to their parents."

Riley M. Greenwood (Kansas '82) writes of shared Delta Chi experiences with his father Jack E. Greenwood (Kansas '49) and his brother Jack M. Greenwood (Kansas '85). "Our house at KU is thought to be haunted by the ghost of a worker that fell from the roof during construction. While at the house alone my father had a strange incident with this ghost, the French doors in the house all began opening and closing. I too had an encounter while standing in nearly the same spot my dad had thirty years earlier, feeling a cold hand gripping the back of my neck."

Thomas B. Gunter (Florida '80) writes with pride about his son, Paul Thomas Gunter (Florida '08). Greatly enjoying his Delta Chi experience at the University of Florida, Gunter was disappointed his son would not have the opportunity to follow his footsteps as the chapter had lost its charter. "As luck would have it, the Chapter was being allowed to return and form a colony during his time at UF. He joined the colony as a Founding Father and became the 'C' on the first Executive Board...I am very proud of my son and the other Founding Fathers, and all the members of successive classes, that have worked hard and so successfully brought our Fraternity back into a prominent position on the UF campus. I am pleased to call my son my Brother."

In May 1937, Dr. Marsh White and Field Secretary Blair organized the first Eastern Regional Conference. Held at Penn State, the conference was essentially officer training for seven eastern chapters. Walter L. Peterson ("A" of Penn State at the time) wrote, "The National Convention is extremely important for it determines national policy and deals with individual chapter problems. However, time, distance, limited attendance, and the importance of problems of the National Fraternity limit the attention that can be given to each chapter. Regional Conferences supplement the National Convention by enabling all the officers of several chapters to meet during the school year for mutual discussion." One hundred seven

Henry V. McGurren posed behind his desk on April 9, 1935, after being named president emeritus of the executive board in honor of his twenty-fifth anniversary as a national Delta Chi officer.

Frank E. Mason (Ohio State '15) worked in various capacities beside John J. Pershing, William Randolph Hearst, and Herbert Hoover.

Director, screenwriter, and producer Leo McCarey (Southern California '17) won his first Academy Award in 1937 for the film *The Awful Truth*. He paired Laurel and Hardy together and directed many memorable films including *An Affair to Remember*. *Courtesy of Paramount Productions, 1935*

DELTA CHI QUARTERLY

Bricker becomes Governor of Ohio
(See page 101)

March 1939

Volume 35 No. 3

John W. Bricker (Ohio State '16) was inaugurated in 1939 as the fifty-fourth governor of Ohio. He appointed two fellow Delta Chis to his administration, Paul L. Selvy (Ohio State '22) and Charles H. Jones (Ohio State '07).

actives and alumni showed up at the second Penn State conference held in April 1938. Attendees of the events heartily recommended other regions establish conferences of their own and the concept quickly spread. The Mid-West Conclave soon met as well as the Pacific Coast Regional Conference, the Ohio State Regional Conference, and the Illinois Regional Conference.

As the decade drew to a close, NYU reported Paul Lynahan ('39) was the five-hundredth initiate since the chapter's establishment in 1891. The executive board directed one field secretary to focus entirely on expansion and a third man was hired for chapter visits. With a unique means of organization, a group of men were hand picked by SMU Delta Chis to form the new Oklahoma Chapter in 1938. Previously chapters had been local fraternities seeking a national charter. Handpicking men with traits of leadership and scholarship fit well into the plan of expansion. Heading into the 1940s, Buc Buchanan (Wisconsin '35) was senior field man with Eric Larson (Illinois '35) and Bill Tubbs (Florida '36) doing the traveling.

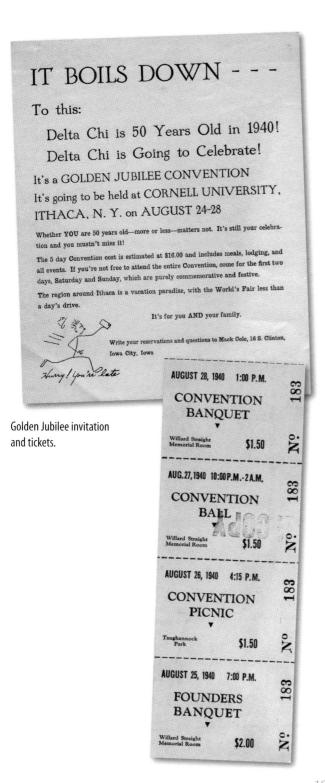

Golden Jubilee invitation and tickets.

> *"Delta Chi has been a long time in the making. Those many years tell countless stories of loyalty and devotion, of actual, not feigned, sacrifice. There have been trying moments, critical periods, but from every one Delta Chi has emerged unwavering and strong."*

QUARTERLY EDITORIAL COMMENT
SEPTEMBER 1940

Delta Chi would celebrate its fiftieth anniversary in 1940 with the twenty-eighth convention held in its birthplace of Ithaca, New York. As convention plans progressed the three living Founders, Peter S. Johnson, Monroe M. Sweetland, and Frederick M. Whitney, all expressed their desire to attend the gathering. "AA" Dean C. M. Thompson (Illinois Faculty) hoped that every chapter would own a home, be self-supporting, and be high in scholarship by the 1940 convention.

A bevy of Delta Chi dignitaries convened at the convention on Sunday, August 25, 1940. Of the fourteen living men who had held the position

Former "AAs" who attended the fraternity's Golden Jubilee were, from left to right, Edward C. Nettels, Harry H. Barnum, John J. Kuhn, Osmer C. Ingalls, Henry V. McGurren, John B. Harshman, and C. M. Thompson.

of "AA," seven gathered in Ithaca. The regrets of Founders Whitney and Johnson were read to the delegates. Whitney wrote, "Regret my inability to be with you at our Golden Jubilee Convention. Kindly extend to all members of Delta Chi my sincere wishes for the happiest of good times, fellowship, and success of this convention." A standing ovation greeted the introduction of Founder Monroe Sweetland. John C. Trussell (Cornell '28) was present to hear Sweetland speak and later wrote of the event, "He suggested all Delts come up and shake hands for what he called 'Hands across the Centuries'…I remember that we all lined up and shook hands with him in the Union Building (Willard Straight Hall)."

On behalf of the entire fraternity, Edward C. Nettels (Chicago-Kent '00, "AA" 1904–05) presented a bronze tablet to the Cornell Chapter in commemoration of the convention. The very popular Dean C. M. Thompson was reelected "AA". After his acceptance speech, "The Dean" received an ovation lasting several minutes. The

The uniforms of Cadet Colonel Carl Miller (Arizona '41) and Cadet Second Lieutenant Herb Stevenson (Arizona pledge) were featured in the March 1941 *Quarterly* portending the entrance of the United States into World War II.

September 1940 *Quarterly* observed, "The Dean has stolen the affection of fraternity audiences everywhere…His faith in Delta Chi has made him a symbol of inspiration throughout the fraternity, and his foresight and wisdom have greatly contributed to the furtherance of the practical program which Delta Chi carried on." Due in part to the absence of conventions during World War II, Thompson was "AA" for seventeen consecutive years, not leaving office until 1952.

Delta Chi entered the new decade with thirty-four chapters and strong representation in Washington. The fraternity claimed three United States Senators—James E. Murray of Montana (NYU '00), Lewis B. Schwellenbach of Washington State (Washington '16), and Matthew M. Neeley of West Virginia (West Virginia '04)—and no less than eight members in the House of Representatives. After ten years in place, the scholarship program continued to produce the desired results. The trophy for ranking first in scholarship was given to Oregon State three times in the decade and DePauw twice. DePauw was proud to have five Phi Beta Kappa members living in its house at one time in the 1940s. C. Woody Thompson (Illinois '22) was the director of scholarship. The conclaves had become an integral part of the fraternity. Donald G. Isett (Kansas '28) was appointed director of conclaves in an attempt to coordinate and unify the groups.

World War II quickly brought the old ways of fraternity life to a halt. Dean Thompson ("AA") wrote in September of 1942, "Delta Chis recognize their duty in this National emergency, and may they act so that it can never be said that a single one of them refused to face that duty, or failed in meeting it fully." At the time the September 1942 *Quarterly* was printed, two brothers were missing in action, Ralph Bennett

(Michigan State '40) and Robert Wuest (Pennsylvania '41). It was soberly noted that eight young men had given the last full measure of devotion for their countries, Emmett Blakemore Jr. (SMU '38), George Gilbert (Arizona '42), Mathew J. Horan (NYU '28), Joseph Kowalski (Illinois '38), Walter B. McManus (Osgoode Hall '38), Robert S. Rogers (Miami '36), Thomas M. Roscoe (Minnesota '34), and Curtis R. Vander Heyden (UCLA '35). This list sadly grew in each successive *Quarterly*. First Lieutenant Spencer P. Edwards (UCLA '40) concluded a letter to his Delta Chi brothers back home, "How do we like it? We're soldiers; that's the only answer."

Lieutenant Jim Brandt (Minnesota '37) told a fantastic story of Delta Chis at war. While flying in the South Pacific, Brandt and seven fellow members of the US Navy Air Corps were separated from their force. They landed on one of the many thousand small islands in the South Pacific. On that island, inhabited only by friendly natives, coconuts, and a few chickens, Brandt encountered his Minnesota roommate William McGowan, who had been recently reported lost at sea. After being stranded for more than two weeks, both men managed to repair their planes and return to their forces.

Seven finely printed pages of the 1942 *Quarterly* were dedicated to a partial list of the over two thousand Delta Chis in active service to the armed forces of the United States and Canada. It was announced, "Due to the War, the Convention scheduled for 1942 has been postponed by vote of the Executive Board of the Fraternity concurred in by vote of the chapters." Delta Chi was a powerful link to home and the promise of peace. Dedicated brothers, like Hillas Eskridge (Oklahoma '42), even remembered to

Dean C. M. Thompson (Illinois faculty) served as "AA" from 1935 until 1952. Thompson was flanked at the 1942 Midwest Regional Conference by O. K. Patton (Iowa '12) on his right and Henry V. McGurren (Chicago-Kent '10) on his left.

HANDS ACROSS THE CENTURIES

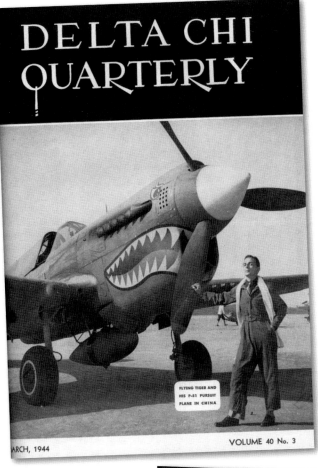

DELTA CHI QUARTERLY

ARCH, 1944   VOLUME 40 No. 3

Above: First Lieutenant Jack A. Blanco (LSU '44) was a Flying Tiger under command of General Chennault in China. He received the Air Medal from the United States government and was awarded the Distinguished Flying Cross for having completed over forty combat missions.

Right: Lieutenant Alex Vraciu Jr. (DePauw '41) finished World War II as the navy's fourth ranking ace. He shot down nineteen Japanese planes, six in one day, and destroyed twenty-one on the ground. Vraciu was named Delta Chi of the Year for 2010.

DELTA CHI QUARTERLY

SEPTEMBER, 1944   ★   VOLUME 41 No. 1

pay their dues. He wrote the executive office from North Africa, "Am enclosing check for alumni dues for '42–43. Due to unforeseen circumstances it will probably be a little late in arriving. I trust that it will do its bit to keep dear old Delta Chi going through the war. It will be a great pleasure to return to the active chapter after the war."

The thirty-seventh chapter, Washington State, was installed on January 16, 1943. Postwar planning for the future of the fraternity was critical. All chapters had lost men and there were few pledges to replace them. Active pledging dropped 90 percent from 1942 to 1943. The quality of rushing was emphasized in a letter to the LSU Chapter by its former "A", Edward Glusman, "Despite the apparent lack of material for pledging in the coming months, be choosy. Pick your men and be sure you are right." The universities leased many chapter houses including Kansas, Alabama, DePauw, Illinois, Indiana, Iowa, Michigan State, Ohio State, Oklahoma, Oregon State, Penn State, Purdue, SMU, and Stanford. These chapter houses were all used to house servicemen.

The executive office became a clearinghouse for all things Delta Chi. The Delta Chi executive secretary was O. K. Patton (Iowa '12), professor of law at the University of Iowa, but the real work of the office was done by Office Manager Bernice Hauber, a receptionist, and two secretaries. They answered scores of letters received from brothers in service. They attempted to maintain accurate rolls and diligently tried to

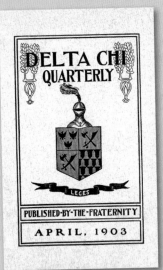

"THAT THE NAME OF THE QUARTERLY PUBLICATION OF THE DELTA CHI FRATERNITY SHALL BE KNOWN AS THE DELTA CHI QUARTERLY."

THE COMMITTEE ON FRATERNITY PUBLICATIONS PRESENTED THIS RESOLUTION TO THE CHICAGO CONVENTION DELEGATES IN 1902. THE EIGHT CHAPTERS REPRESENTED UNANIMOUSLY PASSED THE RESOLUTION AND THE *QUARTERLY* WAS BORN. VOLUME 1, NUMBER 1 WAS PUBLISHED IN 1903 UNDER DIRECTION OF EDITOR HAROLD F. WHITE (CHICAGO-KENT '01). WHITE WAS HANDICAPPED BY THE LACK OF A RELIABLE LIST OF ALUMNI AND ACTIVE MEMBERS. HE LAMENTED THAT ANY FUTURE *QUARTERLY* EDITOR WOULD BE DOOMED WITHOUT THE SUPPORT OF ALUMNI. BY THE TIME THE SECOND EDITION WAS PRINTED, A NEW EDITOR WAS AT THE HELM, JAMES O'MALLEY (CORNELL '01). NINE OTHER EDITORS FOLLOWED O'MALLEY. BEGINNING WITH EDWARD NETTELS (CHICAGO-KENT '00), THERE WERE THIRTEEN BUSINESS MANAGERS OF THE PUBLICATION. IN JANUARY OF 1934, WITH VOLUME XXX, NUMBER 2, THE STAFF OF THE EXECUTIVE OFFICE BEGAN EDITING THE *QUARTERLY* AS WELL AS HANDLING THE BUSINESS SIDE OF THE MAGAZINE.

IN THE BEGINNING THE SUBSCRIPTION RATE WAS $0.50 FOR BOTH ACTIVES AND ALUMNI. IN 1923 THE LIFE SUBSCRIPTION PLAN WENT INTO EFFECT WITH THE SUBSCRIPTION INCLUDED IN THE INITIATION FEE. THE LIFE SUBSCRIPTION RATE WAS INCREASED IN 1952 IN RESPONSE TO RISING PRINTING AND DISTRIBUTION COSTS. EACH EDITION RECOGNIZED *QUARTERLY* "E" KEY WINNERS BECAUSE "THEY WERE PROMPT; BECAUSE THEY SUBMITTED THE MATERIAL REQUESTED; BECAUSE THEIR PICTURES WERE CANDID, NEWSY, AND IN GOOD TASTE; BECAUSE THEY EXCEEDED THE MINIMUM REQUIREMENTS."

THE LOOK OF THE *QUARTERLY*'S COVER CHANGED DRAMATICALLY OVER THE YEARS. THE EARLY YEARS FEATURED VARIOUS INTERPRETATIONS OF THE DELTA CHI COAT OF ARMS. THE FIRST PICTURE COVER WAS OF DON LASH (INDIANA '37) SHOWN SETTING A NEW WORLD'S RECORD FOR THE TWO-MILE RUN. IN 1957 THE FORMAT CHANGED FROM 9 X 12 INCHES TO A MUCH SMALLER 6 X 9. MORE PAGES, SMALLER TYPE, AND THE ELIMINATION OF WHITE SPACE ACTUALLY ALLOWED FOR MORE NEWS IN THE SMALLER EDITIONS.

THE 1949 EXECUTIVE BOARD WELL EXPLAINED THE *QUARTERLY*'S PURPOSE. "THE MAGAZINE DOES NOT BRAG PAGE AFTER PAGE OF THE ILLUSTRIOUS ALUMNI, THE NUMBER OF ALL-AMERICANS, THE NUMBER OF PROFESSORS AND COLLEGE PRESIDENTS, AND THE 'CAPTAINS OF INDUSTRY' WHO ARE MEMBERS OF DELTA CHI. THAT IS LOOKING BACKWARD AND HANGING ONTO THE COAT TAILS OF THOSE WHO HAVE SUCCEEDED. THE *QUARTERLY* IS DESIGNED TO HELP PRODUCE MORE OF THESE MEN IN THE FUTURE, NOT TO SPEND ITS TIME BASKING IN THE GLORY OF THE PAST." ONE HUNDRED YEARS OF THE PUBLICATION WAS RECOGNIZED IN 2003. SIXTY THOUSAND COPIES OF THE 2003 FALL EDITION OF THE *QUARTERLY* WERE PRINTED AND MAILED TO EVERY KNOWN DELTA CHI.

DELTA CHI QUARTERLY

SEPTEMBER, 1945 ★ VOLUME 42 No. 1

President Harry Truman, left, appointed Judge Lewis B. Schwellenbach (Washington '17) to be secretary of labor in April 1945. The two men entered the Senate together in 1935 as freshman senators.

continue collecting alumni dues. In a display of interfraternity comity, the dues of Robert H. Tompkins (SMU '46) arrived in an envelope with a note scrawled on the back. "The original sender evidently dropped this. It was found and is being mailed by a Sigma Nu from Montana and an SAE from Adrian College. Fraternal Greetings." The executive board drafted a plan for chapter rebuilding as soon as the war drew to a close. Delta Chis in the service desperately wanted to return to the chapters as they left them. The executive board did all it could so this would be a reality for returning veterans. Robert A. Cline (Illinois '42) wrote, "Some day we'll all be back and want the same companionship that was ours before the war. I'm sure all of us will do our part to keep Delta Chi with us."

With the end of World War II in 1945 veterans returned and many, under the GI Bill, headed to college campuses. Returning from the Pacific Theatre in May 1946, Warren W. Etcheson received a letter from the executive office inviting him to apply for a position as field secretary. He responded and was hired, without an interview, with a salary of $200 a month. Etcheson wrote a letter to Raymond Galbreth in 2006 describing his field secretary position: "My assignment was to visit as many of the distant chapters as I could in a year, to counsel them in organization and management, to urge local alumni to assist local chapters in reestablishing themselves, and to scout out promising expansion sites." His schedule for 1946 was impressive. "Starting in Minnesota I went out to the chapters of the Pacific Northwest, then down the coast to Los Angeles, across the Southwest to Texas in time for Christmas recess. After Christmas in Iowa City I went back to Texas, then across the southern states to Florida, up the coast to New York, over to Toronto, and back to Iowa City by the end of the academic year. Because cars were difficult to acquire

Sam Lindauer (Stanford '10), on the right, hosted the "Annual Dude Wrangle" on June 15, 1946, and enjoyed his role as sheriff.

Hands Across the Centuries

immediately after WWII, I did all the traveling by train with an occasional bus ride to places not served with convenient train service." Upon his return to Iowa City Etcheson was promoted to administrative secretary and given a raise of $50 a month.

The first postwar regional conference was held in West Lafayette, Indiana, in April 1946. Slowly the *Quarterly*'s pages began to turn from war and again included stories of pranks and parties, formals and football games. As the fraternity looked forward, its last tie to the founding in 1890 was broken. Peter Schermerhorn Johnson, the last surviving Founder, died on September 23, 1947, at the age of seventy-seven. In a tribute to him, the *Quarterly* recorded some of Johnson's thoughts on what Delta Chi meant to him: "The sentiment of the friendship of the founders has passed on through the years to men and the sons of men we never knew. It is queer when you study the matter that you have a feeling of real personal interest in people you never met, from a college you never saw, just because they have subscribed to the same set of ideals as yourself." Delta Chis today continue to feel affinity and gratitude toward Johnson and all the Founders who went before them.

The question of the next convention's date began to circulate in 1948. The delegates last gathered in Ithaca, celebrating the fraternity's fiftieth anniversary, in 1940. The executive board was hesitant. Meeting for the first time postwar in January of 1948, the board questioned that the chapters had reached a level of postwar stability warranting a convention.

The executive board met for an intensive three-day meeting in the fall of 1949. Held at the fraternity headquarters in Iowa City, Iowa, all nine members attended, traveling an aggregate of nearly 18,000 miles to consider topics vital to

Jefferson J. Coleman, right, and Russell C. McFall, left, deplaned in Iowa City on August 30, 1949. They were the first executive board members to arrive for a pivotal three-day meeting.

This executive board meeting included, from left to right, John Harshman, Henry McGurren, Marsh White, Dean C. M. Thompson, Pete Anderson, O. K. Patton (seated), Lewis Armstrong, and "Mac" Cole (seated).

the fraternity's future. Since their last meeting in January 1948, five chapters had been reinstalled or reactivated and another charter petition was pending. The extensive agenda included discussion of internal development, chapter size, house management, expansion, and scholarship. As World War II drew to a close many had tried to return Delta Chi to prewar conditions. The board now considered if a return to the old ways was really best or if an entirely new plan should be considered. They developed a long-range expansion program including four focus areas— the Rocky Mountain Region, Canada, the East and Midwest, and the South. Many chapters had grown too large and scholarship had significantly declined in all fraternities as well as

Delta Chi. A conversation was held noting that there had been no change in fees since the 1915 convention, thirty-four years prior. National Director of Scholarship C. Woody Thompson (Illinois '22) reported scholarship showed no significant signs of improvement and noted, "We have made our contribution to the national disgrace."

The convention was again postponed. The executive board adopted the following motion, "That the 1950 Convention be postponed… and that the funds appropriated and allocated to defray the expenses of holding a convention in 1950 be used to carry out the expansion program adopted by the Board at the recent meeting and to pay the expenses of schools of instruction for chapter officers and the 'BBs'." The decade would end with no plans for a convention on the horizon.

Leo Nomellini (Minnesota '50) enjoyed his time off the gridiron. He was the first draft choice of the San Francisco 49ers when they joined the NFL in 1950. Named to All-NFL teams on both offense and defense, Nomellini was inducted into the Pro Football Hall of Fame in 1969.

CHAPTER SEVEN:
1950–1959

Alvin C. McDaniel (Missouri '50) attended the 1952 Christmas formal at the Missouri Chapter house at 1415 University Avenue in Columbia, Missouri.

This early 1950s gathering included Field Secretary Tom Chisholm (SMU '47), far left; Warren W. Etcheson (Indiana '42), second from left; Charles M. "Mac" Cole (Iowa '37), third from left; and Lewis S. "Lew" Armstrong (Washington '39), far right.

"Can the brothers of today have anything in common with their brothers of the earlier days? I found my question being continually answered. That it was indeed the spirit of Delta Chi; and that we are all brothers; and each one seemed to say, 'Any brother that is good enough for Delta Chi is good enough for me.'"

FOUNDER ALBERT SULLARD BARNES

1911 CONVENTION ADDRESS

The 1950s began with the retirement of a man who in many ways formed the modern incarnation of Delta Chi. In September of 1951, thirty years after his election to the governing board, O. K. Patton (Iowa '12) announced his retirement from fraternity work. "I regret very much that I must ask the board to relieve me of further administrative responsibilities concerning the work of the Fraternity." He resigned the position of executive director, which he had held since 1929. The central office and chapter finance system were both devised and implemented by Patton. Conventions under his guidance became times of great work and accomplishment. He also inspired chapter visits by trained field secretaries. The January 1952 *Quarterly* spoke for all brothers, "We can never repay but we will always remember your selfless devotion to the remaking of Delta Chi as an association of better-trained and better-brained citizens, increasingly creditable to the American college world."

Delta Chis were making their marks on football in the early 1950s. Giles and Connell Miller (SMU '41 and '42 respectively) bought the failed New York Yankee football team and brought the first professional football team to Texas. The Dallas Texans unfortunately had a disappointing season and the Millers, unable to make payroll, returned the team to the league before the season ended. Charles A. "Chuck" Taylor (Stanford '43) made a much more successful gridiron showing. As a student, Taylor played on the undefeated Stanford team of 1940 and on the 1941 team, winning the Rose Bowl over Nebraska. Taylor returned to Stanford as head football coach in 1952. He led his team to the Rose Bowl that first season making him the first person to have participated in the Rose Bowl as both a player and a head coach. The American Football Coaches Association named him Coach of the Year in 1952. At thirty-one he was the youngest coach to receive that honor. Taylor was "A" of the Stanford Chapter in 1943 and "BB" for several years following the war.

With no conventions as cause to gather since 1940, the regional conferences continued to bring large groups of actives and alumni together. In April of 1951 the Northeastern

James P. Pope (Chicago '09) served as the director of the Tennessee Valley Authority from 1939 until 1951. Prior to his appointment to this position by President Franklin D. Roosevelt, Pope served as a United States Senator from Idaho. *Library of Congress*

THE CEREMONIES OF DELTA CHI

THE 1903 CONVENTION ADOPTED THE FIRST PLEDGE "BUTTON," AS IT WAS THEN KNOWN. IT WAS THE DESIGN BEING USED BY CORNELL, DICKINSON, AND MICHIGAN AND WAS DESCRIBED AS A TRIANGULAR BUTTON HAVING A RED BACKGROUND, WITH A BUFF DELTA ENCLOSING A SMALL CHI. ITS COST FROM THE JEWELER WAS $0.75. APPARENTLY, SOME CHAPTERS DEVISED THEIR OWN DESIGN AND THE 1910 CONVENTION RECOMMENDED THE ADOPTION OF THE PIN THE OHIO STATE CHAPTER HAD THEN BEEN USING. ALTHOUGH THERE IS NO RECORD OF ITS DESIGN, THE FRATERNITY'S ARCHIVES CONTAIN TWO POSSIBILITIES: A SMALL TRIANGLE FILLED ENTIRELY WITH RED ENAMEL AND ONE A BIT LARGER WITH A YELLOW BORDER. WHATEVER THE DESIGN, IT ULTIMATELY PROVED UNSATISFACTORY, AS IT WAS TOO SIMILAR TO PINS BEING USED BY OTHER ORGANIZATIONS. THE BOARD ADOPTED THE PRESENT PIN IN 1949 ALONG WITH A NEW PLEDGING CEREMONY. FOR A BRIEF TIME IN THE 1960S, THE FRATERNITY USED A SPECIAL PLEDGE PIN FOR COLONY MEMBERS WHO HAD YET TO BE INITIATED. IT WAS RED WHERE THE REGULAR PIN IS BLACK OR WHITE AND YELLOW WHERE THE RED IS NOW.

THERE WAS NO OFFICIAL PLEDGING CEREMONY UNTIL 1923 WHEN THE TROUTDALE CONVENTION PROPOSED AN OPTIONAL CEREMONY FOR THE CHAPTERS TO CONSIDER AS THE CHAPTERS WERE CLAIMING THEIR SITUATIONS WERE "UNIQUE." THE 1940 CONVENTION MINUTES REPORT ON A LACK OF CONSISTENCY WITH MANY CHAPTERS USING NO CEREMONY AT ALL. ULTIMATELY, THE BASIS FOR THE CURRENT CEREMONY WAS FORMALLY ADOPTED IN 1949. IN THE LATE 1980S, THE BOARD ADOPTED THE VOLUNTARY USE OF "ASSOCIATE MEMBER" IN PLACE OF "PLEDGE."

IN REACTION TO SO MANY ALUMNI STATING, "I WAS A DELTA CHI" AND AN INSUFFICIENT NUMBER OF ALUMNI HELPING THE CHAPTERS, THE BOARD AUTHORIZED THE DEVELOPMENT OF AN "ALUMNI CEREMONY" TO INDICATE A MEMBER'S TRANSITION TO ALUMNUS STATUS AND INCLUDED EACH INDUCTEE PLEDGING HIS CONTINUED INVOLVEMENT. THIS CEREMONY WAS FORMALLY ADOPTED AT A 1993 BOARD MEETING. IN 1997, THE MEMORIAL CEREMONY WAS FORMALLY ADOPTED IN RECOGNITION OF THE FINAL PASSAGE FOR A MEMBER OF DELTA CHI.

Regional Conference resolved, three years ahead of national action on the clause, to delete the requirement that Delta Chi candidates be white. They also resolved to finally hold a convention. The 1952 convention in French Lick, Indiana, was the first opportunity in a decade for Delta Chis from across the continent to mingle. Travel options and accommodations were outlined in the May 1952 *Quarterly*. The opening sentence of the issue summed up the excitement of many in the active forty-one chapters. "Delta Chis everywhere have been waiting for the announcement that is the main feature of this number of the *Quarterly*." With its central location, the convention planners hoped French Lick would lure delegates from both coasts. While this was the first convention for many, several brothers set lifetime attendance records. A. Frank John had attended eighteen conventions in a row. John B. Harshman, the fraternity's legal advisor, made 1952 his sixteenth, followed by Henry V. McGurren who counted the French Lick convention as number fourteen, five of which he served as convention chairman. Marsh W. White (Penn State '20) was elected "AA" at the 1952 convention after serving on the executive board since 1935. Remnants of the 1952 convention remain in the Iowa City headquarters today. Alumnus Reuben T. Carlson (Georgetown '26) presented three ceremonial chairs to the fraternity each depicting the Delta Chi coat of arms. The chairs were shipped in 1954 from Iowa City to Biloxi for use at the thirtieth convention and the "AA"'s chair was also used at the 1990 Centennial Convention in Syracuse, New York. The chairs remain at the headquarters today.

Resigning his position as executive secretary in 1953, Don Isett was replaced by Warren W. Etcheson (Indiana '42). Etcheson had visited all Delta Chi chapters during his years as field secretary and was more than prepared to take on his new role. He wrote a letter to all chapter "As" outlining the convention ritual committee's report, adopted unanimously by the 1952 delegates. His letter began, "There seems to be general agreement that the ritualistic practices of the fraternity have become unfortunately varied. In some chapters, portions of the initiation have degenerated to an occasion for ridicule and jesting." The committee reminded chapters of Delta Chi's leadership in abolishing hazing. The following recommendation was made. "Pre-initiation programs involving exhausting physical exercises, out-of-town hikes, and giving of drugs, designed only to wear down the neophyte, should be omitted from the pledge-training program."

Scholarship continued to be in steady decline. A frustrated C. Woody Thompson (Illinois '22), national director of educational activities, found many ways to describe the gloomy situation. Preparing for the 1952 convention he reported, "Heretofore my annual report has been entitled: Scholarship. For this report, let's

This ceremonial chair has been at headquarters since its donation in 1952.

Warren W. Etcheson (Indiana '42) was executive director from 1953 to 1956.

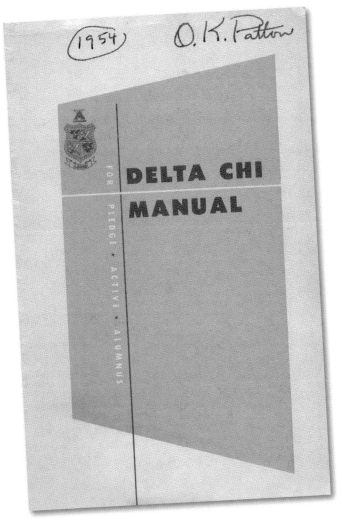

This Delta Chi manual belonged to O. K. Patton (Iowa '12), executive director 1929–51, "CC" emeritus, and member of the Order of the White Carnation.

be realistic and admit that our fraternity has no scholarship worth mentioning…So about all that can be said for our overall performance is that it is a disgrace." Thompson used the Florida Chapter as an example of how to right the situation. In one year, Florida's scholastic ranking on campus soared from twenty-third to first place. "The chapter decided to initiate only men with graduation potential, and to create an environment in the house that would encourage continued good performance… But over and above mechanics is that intangible thing called spirit or attitude. The Florida Chapter evidences a pride in good performance…The first obligation of a Delta Chi there is to do his best and to help his brothers do their best." Thompson hoped this attitude would be catching. Frustrated after fifteen years at the scholarship helm, Thompson attempted resignation saying, "…new blood and new ideas are desperately needed. To get this, I am stepping out." The executive board convinced Thompson to continue in his position.

Delta Chi continued asserting its presence in politics. The 1952 election cycle resulted in two gubernatorial positions for Arizona brothers Governor William G. Stratton of Illinois (Arizona '34) and Governor George N. Craig of Indiana (Arizona '32). President Eisenhower appointed Roger Steffan (Ohio State '13) White House director of operations. Before serving the White House, Steffan served his Ohio State Chapter as "E", "C", and "A", was editor of the *Quarterly*, was a member of the executive board, attended nine conventions, and was the first brother to pay life alumni dues. The fraternity maintained multiple seats in both the United States Senate and House of Representatives. Delta Chis holding state and local offices were far too numerous to note.

The National Interfraternity Conference

This 1999 *Quarterly* cover featured Delta Chis who served as president of the National Interfraternity Conference. Clockwise from the top left are John Kuhn, Charles Gerstenberg, Lewis Armstrong, and Russell MacFall. Gregory Hauser is pictured in the center.

After several years' effort on part of the "XX", Billy Bride proudly reported in the February 1913 *Quarterly* that Delta Chi had been admitted membership to the National Interfraternity Conference (NIC). "I believe that this is a great forward step for Delta Chi. It secures us the recognition for which we have been praying ever since our establishment; it makes us known as exactly what we are in fact — a college fraternity... Delta Chi is indeed fortunate that it is given the opportunity to receive the benefits from association in this Conference and her participation in it will certainly be productive of much good within the fraternity." John J. Kuhn (Cornell '98 and twice serving "AA") was elected president of the conference in 1922. Future Conference President Charles W. Gerstenberg (NYU '04) reported in 1923 the New York Interfraternity Club building was progressing on Madison Avenue and 38th Street. Emblazoned with participating fraternity coats of arms, the Delta Chi coat of arms can still be found on the building today.

Delta Chi was proud when Brother Gerstenberg became chairman of the conference in 1930 and again in 1938 when Russell MacFall (NYU '22) assumed the position of leadership. In 1954, after representing Delta Chi at twenty consecutive annual meetings of the National Interfraternity Conference, Marsh W. White (Penn State '20) became the fourth Delta Chi to hold a seat on the executive committee. It would be nearly twenty years before another Delta Chi would lead the NIC. In December of 1972, at the sixty-third annual conference meeting in St. Louis, Lewis S. Armstrong ("AA" emeritus) was elected president. M. Gary Monk ("AA" emeritus) served on the NIC board during the 1980s.

Delta Chi had supported and supplied leadership for the National Interfraternity Conference since 1913. Fifth Delta Chi President Gregory F. Hauser (Michigan State '75) was installed as conference president on December 5, 1998, and is a recipient of the NIC Gold Medal. In 2009, Charles Mancuso (Florida State '84) was elected to serve on the NIC board. Two Delta Chi chapters have received the NIC's Award of Distinction in the chapter category, George Tech in 2004 and 2010 and Kansas in 2007. In 2012, Delta Chi Executive Director Ray Galbreth (Missouri '69) received the NIC Gold Medal. Delta Chi is tied with three other fraternities for the most men having led the NIC.

Robert J. Zoller (Iowa '38) posed with his world champion Alaskan Malamute Geronimo (Ch. Apache Chief of Husky-Pak) in 1953, the year he took National Capital Show Best of Breed.

Since 1951, the Alabama Chapter has had an Indian Party. Brothers Norman Hahn ('55), John Ed Willoughby ('57), and Clint Miller ('57) enjoyed the 1954 event.

Echoing the tragic Cornell house fire of 1900, the DePauw Chapter lost their house on October 7, 1952. Fortunately, most residents were not home and there was no loss of life. An insurance settlement was worked out for $10,600 for damage to the structure and $5,600 for damage to the house contents. Two weeks after the fire, contractors started to rebuild. All chapters were urged to review their insurance programs and emergency evacuation plans. Issues such as chapter insurance coverage brought the executive board together for a special meeting in September of 1953. Four members of the board—the executive secretary, the director of educational activities, and the two field secretaries—gathered at the Edgewater Beach Hotel in Chicago. The men debated a comprehensive investment strategy, incorporation of the fraternity, and planned for the next convention.

Shortly after this special meeting, Marsh W. White ("AA") announced that the thirtieth international convention would be held at the Buena Vista Hotel in Biloxi, Mississippi, over Labor Day weekend 1954. For the first time in the fraternity's sixty-four years, delegates would convene in the Deep South. Single rooms would be $4 a day with the rate for a suite increasing to $17. Many delegates headed to Biloxi with the newly printed *Delta Chi Manual* in hand. Enlarged to one hundred pages from the previous eighty, the manual was designed to help the pledge, the member, the chapter officer, and the alumnus. It was noted in the *Quarterly*, "Manuals, particularly pledge manuals have the disturbing habit of being nothing more than compendium of historical facts which become the rule book for an interesting game in which the pledge counselor attempts to make these dry facts palatable enough for pledge consumption – by force feeding or otherwise." The new manual was written with hopes of being more than

This map was used at the 1954 convention to illustrate active chapters and the nine regional divisions created at that gathering.

The 1954 convention was held in Biloxi, Mississippi.

that. The compilers did not claim to be the final word on fraternity history. "It will remain as the task of those who follow to broaden further the scope of this *Manual* and elaborate in more detail the program of Delta Chi Fraternity."

Despite slow movement to improve scholastics fraternity wide, Delta Chi of the 1950s boasted more than its share of leaders in academia. Eight college presidents had been active Delta Chis during their own undergraduate years. J. Whitney Bunting (Pennsylvania '34) was president of Oglethorpe University in Atlanta. William V. Houston (Ohio State '20)

became president of Rice in 1946 and Cloyd H. Marvin (Stanford '13) was at the helm of George Washington University for over thirty years. Earl J. McGrath (Buffalo '28) became president of the University of Kansas City in 1954 and Ellwood C. Nance (Rollins faculty) led the University of Tampa. Peyton N. Rhodes (Virginia '20) had been president of Southwestern College of Memphis since 1949, Hedrick B. Young (Indiana '25), was the president of Western College for Women, and Noah N. Langdale Jr. (Alabama '41) was appointed president of the Georgia State College of Business in 1957.

Many captains of industry were brothers as well. W. P. "Bill" Klapp (Penn State '24) headed Original Sight-Exchange Company, at the time the largest distributor of gun sights in the world. S. Clark Beise (Minnesota '22) became president of the Bank of America, the world's

Delta Chi claimed first place in the 1954 Alabama Homecoming Parade.

In the fall of 1954 Doug King, Bill Clark, and Rob McGregor proudly installed the Delta Chi insignia on their recently remodeled Southern California Chapter house.

The 1955 Western Michigan chartering drew notable Delta Chi "AAs" including front row, Henry McGurren, far left; Joe Lacchia, third from left; John Harshman, fourth from left; back row, L. Orville "Swede" Edlund, third from right; and Edward Nettels, fourth from right. *Photo courtesy of Gary B. Walters*

John Harshman (Ohio State '07, "AA" 1929–35), left, made a presentation at the Western Michigan chartering ceremony in 1955 to Ivan Crawford (Western Michigan "A"). *Photo courtesy of Gary B. Walters*

The University of Alabama Delta Chi Student Chapter, directed by Sam Wells (Alabama '55), won the 1955 IFC Step Singing Contest. The fraternity used their recording of the "Bond Song" for many years.

largest bank at the time, on April 1, 1954. Beise revolutionized banking by introducing the first successful bank credit card and a modern system of computer check processing. While at the University of Minnesota Beise held the positions of "A", "B", and "F" in his chapter and was a member of the varsity football team.

The Delta Chi Educational Foundation was incorporated in November 1954. The foundation provided an opportunity for alumni and friends of Delta Chi to aid undergraduate and graduate students who deserved and needed financial assistance. A board of five directors was established. The first men to hold this position were Dean Charles M. Thompson (Illinois Faculty), Roger Steffan (Ohio State '13), John B. Harshman (Ohio State '07), L. Harold "Pete" Anderson (Minnesota and Stanford '24), and Donald G. Isett (Kansas '28). Their first order of business was to draw up bylaws for the foundation. Thompson drafted a letter to all alumni beginning, "The Delta Chi Educational Foundation has no past, but it has a glorious future and that future depends on the support it has from alumni. To carry out any program worthy of our organization, we must have funds in substantial amounts." The first foundation scholarships were awarded in 1957.

The first New England chapter was installed in 1955. The University of Connecticut became the site for the forty-first active chapter with Southern Illinois quickly following as the

This fall of 1955 Alabama rush event included Richard Shelby (Alabama '57), seated at the far right. First elected to the United States Senate in 1986, Shelby is now Alabama's senior senator.

Brothers gathered at the thirty-first Delta Chi convention in 1956 to celebrate sixty-five years of Delta Chi.

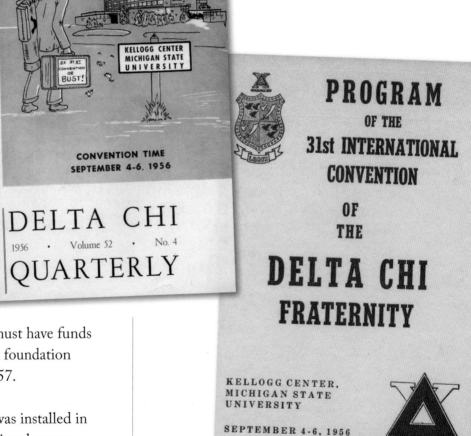

The 1956 convention attendees.

A pledge pin was presented to Robert "Bob" Cauthen (Auburn '59) in 1956. Lawrence L. Norman (Auburn '58) congratulates Cauthen while Rush Chairman John "Skeeter" Tapley (Auburn '56) attaches the pin to his lapel.

R. Harrison "Stork" Sanford (Washington '26) successfully coached the Cornell crew for thirty-four years. His 1957 team was undefeated and broke a 118-year-old record when they won the Henley Royal Regatta Grand Challenge Cup.

forty-second. A regional expansion program, the most extensive and intensive since World War II, was in full swing. Celebrating the fraternity's sixty-fifth anniversary, the 1956 convention was held in Michigan, the state of the first Delta Chi convention. One hundred and fifty Delta Chis and their guests were in attendance. It was a pleasure for the director of educational activities to finally report that most chapters were showing academic improvement. The headquarters' council was appointed at the convention to place "in the hands of small

committees the problems which are now facing the General Fraternity." This intimate group was to serve the central office much as a control board served an individual chapter. There was no executive secretary at the helm until 1961. The council members included C. Woody Thompson (Illinois '22), Donald G. Isett (Kansas '28), and O. K. Patton. Their first charge was to increase alumni participation, and their efforts brought success. The Greater Kansas City Delta Chi Alumni Association reported 150 attendees at their 1957 banquet and 96 Los Angeles alumni gathered for dinner. For the first time in fraternity history, Delta Chi had three "AAs" emeriti. Henry V. McGurren, Dean C. M. Thompson, and John B. Harshman shared the honor.

Delta Chi brothers entertained with great style. Duke Ellington and his orchestra were brought in for a dance hosted by the Western Illinois Chapter in 1958. Over eight hundred couples

attended, each leaving with an autographed copy of Ellington's latest recording. Not to be outdone, the Southern Illinois Chapter sponsored a Count Basie concert. The Washington Chapter made a big splash on the social scene when they built Delta Chi's first chapter swimming pool. The Seattle Alumni Association funded the 20 x 40 foot heated pool. With all its social advantages, disadvantages presented themselves as well. Jealousy led to some minor vandalism and the pool offered great distraction from academics. "Strict rules of pool behavior have been established… Pool hours have had to be set; the pool has been placed out of bound for all seventy-five Delta Chis during study hours." The chapter reported that sorority women seemed to be most impressed with the addition. University rules, however, forbade girls to visit fraternities for more than ten minutes without a chaperone, allowing little time for a swim.

The 1958 convention was held at Lake Texoma, near Durant, Oklahoma.

The last convention of the decade was held in 1958 at Lake Texoma Lodge on the Texas-Oklahoma border. Following the directives of the convention to spend time with each chapter, the field representatives traveled 40,000 miles during the 1958–59 school year to visit all forty-five chapters. Depending on circumstances, some chapters warranted second or even third visits. The field men reported on the breadth of their positions: "At various times during the performance of our duties we are called upon to be a psychologist, accountant, socialite, analyst, trouble shooter, junior executive, editor, salesman, traveler, counselor, and expert on any and all subjects related in any manner, direct or remote to fraternities."

The constitution and bylaws were amended at the 1958 convention to establish a more effective geographical organization giving equitable representation among the chapters on the executive board. Duly elected regional representatives, who became members of the board, now supervised regional areas. Charles M. Thompson ("AA" emeritus) wrote, "A year ago every member of the Board could have come from the same community; now, that is impossible. A year ago a majority of the Board resided in three middle-west states; now that is unlikely." Nominees were selected from alumni within the region. Andrew R. MacMillan, chairman of the 1959 "XX", wrote the "BBs", "Let's get ourselves together, at least regionally, and before the next convention. It will benefit you, your Chapters and ultimately the Fraternity. If our beloved Fraternity would grow stronger, this getting together of Chapter Advisors is surely an obvious need and an inevitable blessing for Delta Chi." MacMillan signed off, "Good going, good gatherings, good luck and goodbye."

A 1958 *Quarterly* featured this beguiling convention invitation.

Rod Dedeaux (Southern California '35, past chapter "A") was named college Baseball Coach of the Year in 1958. Coaching USC from 1942 until 1986, his teams won eleven College World Series titles. He coached the US Olympic baseball teams in 1964 and 1984. Dedeaux was the coach for the actors and ballplayers in the 1989 movie *Field of Dreams*, featuring fellow Delta Chi, Kevin Costner.

Four Purdue Delta Chis met with Vice President Richard Nixon in 1959 as representatives of the Purdue Young Republicans.

CHAPTER EIGHT:
1960–1969

33rd INTERNATIONAL CONVENTION

DELTA CHI FRATERNITY

HOTEL SEVERIN
INDIANAPOLIS, IND.
AUG. 31 - SEPT. 2

"Delta Chi is going to have to run faster and faster just to keep in the race at all!"

GEORGE E. OSBORNE (PURDUE '39)
DIRECTOR OF EDUCATIONAL ACTIVITIES

The decade of the 1960s began with the approval of expanding at Texas Western, New Mexico State, and Northern Illinois. The latter two would actually occur many years later. Campuses were beginning to rumble with anti-fraternity sentiment but new Delta Chi houses were being purchased, rush season was busy, and pledge numbers were strong. The *Quarterly* devoted an issue to the concept of public relations and what it meant to fraternities.

Editor Walter Barbee wrote, "Fraternities have realized that they too must develop public relations programs to counter the vicious criticism to which they have been subjected… Probably the most important fraternity public relations activity must be practiced on the chapter level. With this in mind, it would be the duty of the officers of each chapter to determine the local needs of a P.R. program, and then set out to put such a program in operation." The fraternity's living membership was now 17,500. Deceased members numbered close to 3,000 putting total membership solidly over 20,000.

One hundred and fifty delegates from forty-five active chapters and eight alumni chapters convened at the Hotel Severin in Indianapolis for the thirty-third international convention in 1960. The officers elected in 1960 were repeatedly referred to as "the three big men." "Whichever way it came about, probably at no time in the history of Delta Chi have the offices of 'AA,' 'CC,' and 'DD' at any one time been filled by men of such similar stature." Not just referring to the physical size of Claude B. Layfield Jr. (Auburn '46), L. Harold Anderson (Minnesota-Stanford '24), and Lewis S. Armstrong (Washington '39), the three were all largely successful in their fields and were equally devoted to Delta Chi. At this convention the executive committee consisting of the "AA", the "CC", and the "DD" was established and given administrative authority between conventions. This authority included the granting and revoking of chapter charters. In what was remembered as a night of inspiration, Dean C. M. Thompson addressed the convention as guest speaker. He pleaded with the delegates "to keep the long-range objectives of the Fraternity in mind and push ahead during the next biennium."

Henry M. "Scoop" Jackson (Washington '34) was chairman of the Democratic National Committee in 1960. He was a member of the United States Congress, as a representative and senator, from 1941 until his death in 1983. *Photographer Fabian Bachrach*

Due to a constitutional change at convention, the legislative power between conventions was now divorced from the executive and administrative authority. It was hoped that the frustrations of administering the daily affairs of Delta Chi would now pass. The administrative details of the fraternity would solely be falling on the small executive committee, appointed by the executive board. This change further necessitated filling the position of executive secretary, a position vacant for four years. It was not filled until the fall of 1961 when Harold E. "Buc" Buchanan (Wisconsin '35) was hired as the fraternity's first full-time paid executive secretary. Buchanan filled the position until his untimely death in 1966. Dr. F. Kenneth Brasted (Florida '35) was named executive secretary in 1967. Working with limited resources, Brasted

The "call board" was a familiar feature in most Delta Chi houses.

"House Decs," like this one at the Illinois Chapter, have long been an important part of Delta Chi life.

brought great organization to the fraternity and developed manuals for all officers' positions.

Even with memories of World War II fading, Delta Chis were often reminded of the roles brothers played in the Allies' efforts. Colonel Alton C. Miller (Penn State '26) was the head of the United States Army Criminal Investigation Division in 1946. It was in January of that year that Princess Sophia of Greece and Denmark reported the theft of the Hesse-Kassel family jewels. The jewels, valued at several million dollars, had been hidden in the floor of the Hesse family Kronberg Castle, outside of Frankfurt, Germany. After Allied occupation, the United States Army quickly requisitioned Kronberg Castle for a troop rest-and-recreation facility. Regrettably, a band of US Army officers

then pulled off one of the most lucrative wartime thefts in history. Colonel Miller's men tracked down the thieves and recovered much of the treasure. Three of the conspiring officers were convicted of theft by the army and were sentenced to prison. Brother Miller, fluent in French, Spanish, German, Italian, Greek, and Latin, retired from active duty in the provost marshal's office in 1947. He served for a year under Secretary of Defense James Forrestal before finishing his career as a teacher in the Arlington County, Virginia, public school system. Miller, an active Delta Chi alumnus, was a strong supporter of the Penn State Chapter Alumni Association. He spearheaded building the chapter's new house and was honored by a plaque in the clubroom for many years after his death in 1960.

As a new decade began, the fraternity lost its oldest member, Edward C. Nettels (Chicago-Kent '00). Initiated in January of 1896, Nettels attended his first convention in 1900. He lived to see sixty-two years of Delta Chi membership. Nettels said the happiest and most memorable event occurring during his term as "AA" was the installation of the chapter at Leland Stanford University in 1905. He cherished a letter he received from Alden Danner, "A" of Stanford at the time of its installation, fifty-three years later. "It is needless to state how many hundreds of young men have been influenced during the last half century by that event in 1905 at which you officiated. It is also needless to estimate how greatly you and the Fraternity are appreciated for your influence upon their lives."

Russel B. Nye (Wisconsin '33), 1945 Pulitzer Prize winner, kept a close eye on the trends of American culture. He studied all aspect of American life from comic strips and hairstyles to Civil War battles and jazz. Nye once commented, "I keep up with cheap literature

Edward C. Nettels (Chicago-Kent 1900, "AA" 1904–05) was Delta Chi's oldest member when he passed away in 1962.

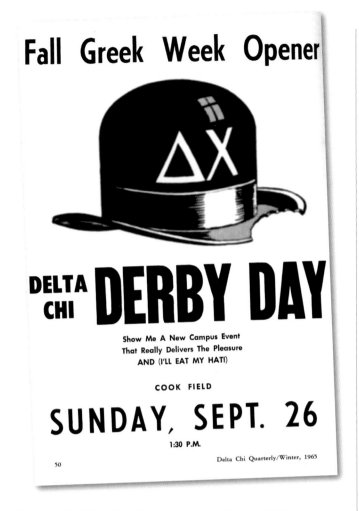

Fall Greek Week Opener

ΔX

DELTA
CHI DERBY DAY

Show Me A New Campus Event
That Really Delivers The Pleasure
AND (I'LL EAT MY HAT!)

COOK FIELD

SUNDAY, SEPT. 26

1:30 P.M.

50   Delta Chi Quarterly/Winter, 1965

The University of Miami Delta Chis celebrated Derby Day in the 1960s.

Indiana brothers formed a pyramid in 1964.

omnivorously. You never know when you'll find something of interest or importance or just plain fun." The 1960s were a time of great changes in American culture impacting all, including fraternities. Coats and ties at dinner were disappearing as well as the services of full-time housemen. Ray Galbreth (Missouri '69) summed up the decade by saying, "Housemothers went out the back door and kegs came in the front." Most brothers were politically aware and struggled with the many issues at hand. Alumni groups were strong nationally and campus reunions helped keep Delta Chi traditions alive even in the tumultuous wake of the times.

In 1963 William A. Anderson Jr. (Kansas '64) and Kirk Bond (Kansas '63) organized a group of women into Chi Delphia. Florida State started the Sisters of the White Carnation and wrote an initiation for them. The chapter selected one girl from each sorority on campus to help the chapter with rush and to represent the fraternity back in their houses. The Florida Chapter, and their Little Sisters, helped spread the program to other campuses. A Wayne State member wrote, "It seems we have never been without little sisters. It is hard to believe they have only been in existence for but one year." The Little Sisters program was addressed at the 1966 convention and was officially adopted. The Little Sisters groups all became known as Chi Delphia and spread to other chapters including San Diego State, Mississippi State, and Texas. George Obear, Delta Chi's legal advisor at the time, remarked, "You will live to regret this." As he predicted, complications grew more frequent through the decades. At the centennial convention in 1990, Delta Chi banned all women's auxiliary groups.

It had been twenty years since the first official regional leadership conference was held. The program continued to promote fellowship and

awareness of fraternity issues. As the sixties began the United States and Canada were divided into eight subdivisions, called regions, with a regional representative responsible for the fraternity activities and programs in his region. The Delta Chi Constitution required regional meetings to be held prior to conventions for election of the representatives. The 1962 convention, held in Colorado Springs, changed the name of the Delta Chi Executive Board to the Board of Regents. The Delta Chi Housing Fund was established to replace the Building Loan Fund. The revision provided for the assessment of each undergraduate chapter $10.00 annually for each member. The fund was used to promote the expansion program and to provide financial assistance to chapters and colonies in securing chapter housing. The convention also provided for a fraternal legal advisor, leading to the appointment of George W. Obear to this position. Dr. Jimmie J. "Doc"

Delta Chi members of the National Interfraternity Conference posed in December of 1964. They included then "AA" Claude Layfield (Auburn '46), first row center; future "AA" Ralph Prusok (Union '52), second row, far left; former "AA" Lewis Armstrong (Washington '39), second row, second from left; and Harold E. "Buc" Buchanan (Wisconsin '35), back row, left, executive director from 1961 to 1966.

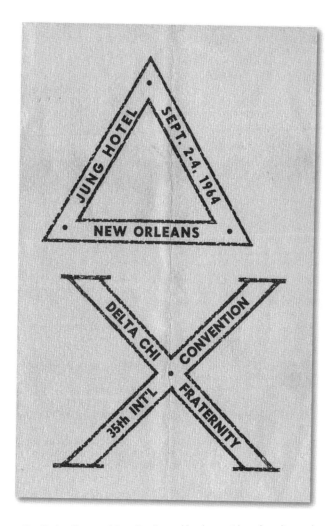

The Mother Chapter of Cornell welcomed brothers to Ithaca for a diamond jubilee celebration in 1965.

Cornell Chapter's Diamond Jubilee

Mail to: Cornell Delta Chi, Diamond Jubilee, 102 The Knoll, Ithaca, New York 14850.

From (Name) ....

Address ....

....

Chapter and Year ....

I wish reservations for myself and .... guests.

Will you need accommodations? ....

Tickets for Cornell-Harvard game ......
@ $4.00 each = $........

Donation for ...... banquet reservations
@ $15.00 each = $........

Checks should be payable to Cornell Delta Chi to cover total.

Underwood (Kansas '51) recalled the 1962 convention "was held in an old wooden hotel downtown that had been built for a reunion of the Grand Army of the Republic in the 1890s… We got enough members sober enough to put on the ritual and spent most of the rest of the night voting to establish the fine points of the ceremony…The next convention I attended was held in New Orleans in 1964 at the Jung Hotel. It was another rat trap." Both hotels were representative of the fraternity's then scarce financial resources.

Delta Chi welcomed its fiftieth and fifty-first chapters in 1965 and on October 13 of that year celebrated its seventy-fifth anniversary. Alumni and actives alike were invited to Cornell for a weekend of reflection and celebration. Preparing for the 1966 convention, the phrase resounded, "Delta Chi is on the go and on the grow!" The fifty-second chapter was installed at Troy State College. The number of chapters jumped to sixty-one chapters by the winter of 1966. The fraternity was shocked by the sudden death of Executive Director Harold E. Buchanan on December 28, 1966. While recognizing a debt to Buchanan's dedication to Delta Chi, the search was on again for an executive director. Dr. F. Kenneth Brasted (Florida '35) was offered the position in June of 1967.

The fall 1967 volume of the *Quarterly* was dedicated to the memory of O. K. Patton (Iowa '12) and John B. Harshman (Ohio State '37). "The deaths, on July 18, 1967 of Odis Knight Patton and, on August 30, 1967, of John B. Harshman, took from the ranks of living Delta Chis two men who will long be remembered for their dedication to the Fraternity which they both loved." As it had during World War I and World War II, editions of the magazine were sent to military men serving around the world. Lieutenant Richard Horton (Florida '66) wrote,

"I am prompted to write this letter because I just received the Summer '67 *Delta Chi Quarterly*. All the articles and pictures brought back to me many memories of things which I took for granted at the time, as you probably do now, but which I now consider a sort of apex of good time…though I [complained] about numerous things, I can truthfully say that the worst times I had in Gainesville are better than the best times here in Vietnam."

A somber quote, familiar to all *Quarterly* readers, was a prelude to more deaths in Vietnam. "These men have lived amongst us for a time, and we have been privileged to call them Brothers. Now they have gone, and we bid them a fond farewell at this parting." Steven Eric Emrick (Alabama '69) was killed in action February 16, 1968. His mother shared his last letter with the *Quarterly*. "Believe me, the U.S. is completely justified in being here. If I die here, I think it will be for a useful and worthy cause." The Viet Cong captured Mike Benge (Oregon State

David Smith (Tulane '65) shot a perfect 100 out of 100 contributing to his team's 1965 world skeet championship victory and the setting of a new world record with their team score of 496 out of 500.

Illinois Delta Chis took starring roles in a 1966 homecoming production.

Mayor Charles Wright Jr. (Kansas '41) of Topeka, Kansas, showed President Johnson damage caused by Topeka's devastating tornado of June 8, 1966.

"AA" David A. Gillespie (Illinois '27) returned to the Illinois Chapter house for dinner in 1967.

'57) on his third tour of duty in Vietnam. His mother relayed, "They say Mike is O.K… We can only hope and pray he will be released soon." G. Keith Phoenix (Southern Illinois Chapter "A") initiated a nationwide campaign of letter writing to the troops. Phoenix realized fraternity members had their individual thoughts about the war. He explained, "The point of the project was not to support the policy of the present administration, but to support the men who are there."

The last convention of the decade was held in Chicago. Delegates met at the Sheraton in August of 1968 to elect the officers that would carry them into the 1970s. Fifty-four chapters were represented with 244 members and guests in attendance. Committees reported the assets of the Delta Chi Educational Foundation totaled $42,810 and the Building Fund had twelve loans outstanding totaling $59,704. This convention added a paragraph to the constitutional section on eligibility for membership stating, "No male student shall be denied membership to an undergraduate chapter because of race, color, creed, religion or national origin." There was not unanimous approval of this addition. A *Quarterly* article was titled, "You Catch It If You Don't and It's No Better If You Do." On one side of the page was a letter criticizing Delta Chi for not leading in integration. On the opposing side of the page was a letter responding to a request for alumni dues: "Only if Delta Chi fights integration." As in society as a whole, Delta Chi would continue to adjust to changing times.

In December 1968 Delta Chi became the owner of a headquarters office building for the first time in the fraternity's history. Sixteen and one half South Clinton Street was an address memorized by hundreds of pledge classes since 1929. That space was always rented and was

Delta Chis Lost in Vietnam

The history of Delta Chi is suffused with young men honorably serving their country. Those who paid the ultimate price continue to be source of pride for the brotherhood. In 1999, Brother George L. Hopkins (Iowa State '61) took upon himself the enormous task of attempting to identify all Delta Chis lost in the Vietnam War. This project was prompted by his desire to remember the name of a brother he had met while serving in Vietnam. He heard this Delta Chi had been killed a few months after they met and remembers receiving this news as a low point of his tour of duty. As time passed Hopkins was appalled he had forgotten the man's name. In an attempt to refresh his memory he contacted Ray Galbreth at headquarters and asked for a list of brothers lost in Vietnam. No such list existed.

Hopkins and Galbreth attempted to change that. Galbreth compiled a list of one thousand brothers who died during the Vietnam era. Hopkins cross-referenced this list against a variety of Vietnam veterans' websites including a list of all casualties, numbering over 64,000. With an enormous amount of time and heart Hopkins' efforts resulted in twelve names, including Robert L. "Bob" Miller (Washington State '58), the name he had lost to time. This type of dedication to fellow Delta Chis, and the fraternity in general, ensures the bond will continue and brothers will not be forgotten.

Edward J. Massare (Cornell '63), left, and Carter J. Nelson (Indiana '67), right, were only two of the many Delta Chis serving their country.

Hands Across the Centuries

DELTA CHI
Quarterly

Summer/Fall 2008

DELTA CHI'S SECRET HERO
JACK WEEKS - ALABAMA '55

On June 4, 1968, Jack Weeks (Alabama '55) died flying an A-12 Blackbird over the South China Sea. Brother Weeks flew CIA reconnaissance missions over Europe and Asia. Information about Weeks's missions and his death was not released until 2007. Family and friends, including his Delta Chi roommate Dan Saltsman (Alabama '56), gathered in 2008 to celebrate this secret hero's life.

not large enough to handle the modern organization's needs. Title to 314 Church Street passed to Delta Chi on December 23, 1968. Built in 1890, ironically the year of the fraternity's founding, the house featured a three-story octagonal tower. The move into the new headquarters was scheduled for July 1, 1969, after major refurbishment. The new building would have offices for the Delta Chi Education Foundation, the *Quarterly*, the executive secretary, and the field staff. A combination library and conference room would fill a long-felt void. The building was officially dedicated on August 16, 1969. In 1993, an addition was added that included a conference room, a storage room, and an expanded entry.

The cynical report of Illinois's "E" Allen Witkowski reflected the unrest as the decade drew to a close. "To keep the traditionalists happy, that is, those who are interested in climbing the frivolous rungs of the Greek social ladder on campus, we picked our house sweetheart from a sorority with many good-looking girls, Delta Delta Delta…As I said before, the preceding was to content those interested in keeping our campus

Twenty-first Hereditary Chief of the Clan McBain, Hughston McBain (Michigan '24) posed at the gate of the McBain Memorial Park, near Inverness, Scotland, on August 30, 1967. McBain was chairman of the board at Marshall Fields.

John M. Burns (Eastern Illinois '69) signed with the Atlanta Braves in 1968.

These were the goals set by the 1968 convention.

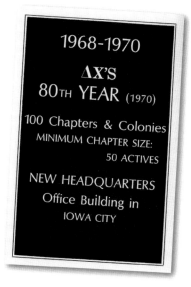

1968-1970

ΔX'S
80TH YEAR (1970)

100 Chapters & Colonies
MINIMUM CHAPTER SIZE:
50 ACTIVES

NEW HEADQUARTERS
Office Building in
IOWA CITY

The fraternity bought and refurbished 314 Church Street in Iowa City for use as its headquarters office building in 1968. This remains the location of Delta Chi Headquarters in 2012.

HANDS ACROSS THE CENTURIES

social rating up and supposedly maintain our all important image." Anti-national sentiments were expressed in the same tone. A letter from Florida read in part, "A change has to be made. The Florida Chapter has become concerned with the inefficient organization of our National structure. We feel a great deal of money is being paid by the undergraduate chapters and colonies into a giant paper-shuffling and letter writing Headquarters Office." They suggested that with the "mood of the undergraduate chapter" maybe a "young, imaginative Executive Director would be beneficial."

Ed Evers (Fullerton '69) posed with the coat of arms.

Headquarters was proudly dedicated in 1969. Shown, left to right, are Frank Granat (Washington '31), George W. Obear (DePauw '30), Ralph E. Prusok (Union '52), Dr. F. Kenneth Brasted (Florida '35), and Dr. Marsh W. White (Penn State faculty).

"Delta Chi stands today as a strong part of the fraternity system. It is like a sleeping giant coming to life. Its body is strong and vibrant. Its muscles are flexed and ready. The blood which courses through its veins and arteries is the blood of thousands of young college men throughout our land, who are breathing into Delta Chi a future of untold growth and prosperity."

CHARLES WRIGHT JR. (KANSAS '41, "CC" 1966–68)

In 1970 the thirty-eighth international convention was held in Dallas, Texas. A small but significant action of this convention was eliminating the eighty-five-year-old requirement that every member purchase a badge. The fraternity and American society were rapidly changing. While Delta Chis in the 1960s collected letters for service men in Vietnam, brothers in the 1970s collected *Playboy* magazines for the troops. Georgia's chapter sponsored a month-long *Playboy* drive, sending letters to every fraternity and sorority on campus requesting assistance and running bi-hourly radio announcements of the drive. At the end of the second week, over one thousand magazines had been collected. They wrote, "The main objective of the magazine drive was to, in some small way, help boost the morale of our troops in Vietnam." It is doubtful any of the collection reached Brother William M. "Bill" Tschudy (SMU '58) or Brother Samuel Robert Johnson (SMU '51). As of publication of the May 1970

This sign on US 12 welcomed visitors to Wisconsin-Whitewater in 1972.

Hands Across the Centuries

Youngstown Brothers Garry Miller ('72) and Mike Monda ('72) made an impressive showing in the 1970 Ugly Man Contest.

Bill Tschudy (SMU '57) was welcomed home in 1972 after being a prisoner of war for over five years.

Quarterly the two men had been prisoners of war by the North Vietnamese for over five years. Tschudy and Johnson returned home safely in 1972. The *Quarterly* warmly welcomed them back to the bond of Delta Chi. Johnson, a decorated war hero, now represents Texas's Third District in the United States Congress.

One Delta Chi had a front row seat for history. Herbert G. "Herb" Klein (Southern California '40) was the first director of White House communications. A long-time friend of President Nixon, Klein worked on Nixon's first congressional campaign in 1946 and all of his later campaigns, eventually bringing them both to the White House in 1969. Klein was at Nixon's side during his historic meetings with Soviet Premier Nikita Khrushchev and traveled with Nixon to China in 1972. With the president embroiled in the Watergate controversy, Klein quit his White House job and returned to journalism on a less public stage. Staff was changing at Delta Chi as well. Executive Director Dr. F. Kenneth Brasted resigned effective June 30, 1975. With the 1975 convention quickly approaching, the executive committee immediately began searching for Brasted's replacement. Their ad read, "This is an excellent opportunity for a person who has a love for the Fraternity and executive ability."

The 1975 convention was held at the Palmer House Hotel in Chicago. Beer stags now topped the list of activities. Like the smokers of the early conventions, Delta Chis gathered to socialize and catch up before the real convention work began. James C. Steffan, "AA" and younger brother of influential *Quarterly* editor Roger Steffan (Ohio State '13), opened the first general session on August 15. He addressed the convention with his state of the fraternity message. He began, "Greeting to our friends in Delta Chi Brotherhood. At this

40th Convention in the 85 years of history of Delta Chi you are attending the largest meeting this Fraternity has ever enjoyed. We have 276 delegates representing 65 chapters, 4 colonies, and 8 alumni chapters." Tragically Brother Steffan suddenly passed away in his hotel room the following day, August 16, 1975.

The "AA" following Steffan was M. Gary Monk (Auburn '65). Returning from two tours of duty as a helicopter pilot in Vietnam, Monk was determined to put Delta Chi back in first-class order. He organized the effort to standardize procedures including the ritual.

A significant action of the 1975 convention was the establishment of the Order of the White Carnation. George W. Obear (DePauw '30), speaking for the board of regents, explained the bylaws provided for the recognition of meritorious and conspicuous service to the fraternity with the designation of officers emeritus. He pointed out that no award, however, provided for the recognition of meritorious and inconspicuous service. "We

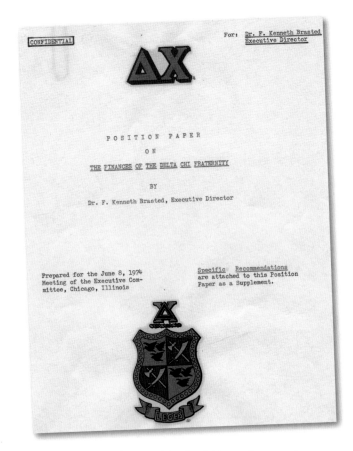

Executive Director Brasted presented this detailed financial report to the executive committee on June 8, 1974. He prepared the committee members beforehand, "I believe this may be the most significant Executive Committee meeting held since I became Executive Director nearly seven years ago."

The 1975 convention was held at the Palmer House in Chicago.

James C. "Jim" Steffan (Ohio State '22, AA 1973–75) spoke to convention delegates the night before he passed away.

In 1975 Victor T. Johnson (Purdue '32) was the first recipient of the Order of the White Carnation. George Obear wrote the OWC charge specifically with Johnson in mind.

hope and suggest that through future experience and tradition the Order of the White Carnation may become more than a treasured award and become an honorary degree of the fraternity. An open and informal degree, no secret, but honored highly." Obear announced the first award of the Order of the White Carnation was given to Victor T. Johnson (Purdue '32), chairman of the educational foundation at the time. The award was presented thrice more before the decade's end, posthumously to James C. Steffan in 1975, to Douglas S. Holsclaw (Arizona '25) in 1977, and to Dr. Marsh W. White in 1979.

While conventions and regional conferences continued to be opportunities for Delta Chis to gather for fraternity business, the Cornell brothers, led by social chairman Dave Read ('78), thought they should have more opportunities to come together simply for fun. On September 23, 1977, brothers from five chapters gathered for a unique weekend to "Roll on the Knoll." Eighty-four members from Cornell, Gorham State, California State, University of Massachusetts, and Hobart made merry from Friday to Sunday and left making plans for their next social gathering. Alumni participation, both monetarily and personally, was at an all time low. A "DD" report to the board of regents in August 1975 outlined one aspect of the financial picture. "Based on strict interpretation of accounting reports Delta Chi has not performed well. But as with any service enterprise where profit is not the motive, accounting does not lend itself to presenting an adequate picture of what has or has not been accomplished. Our goal is to use all our resources in serving the Fraternity. Therefore a large surplus would indicate we were not providing these services and a large deficit would indicate we are providing too many." Alumni participation headed the issue list in 1975 for

Pinned with Pride

A lost Delta Chi pin found its way home in the 1980s. Three decades earlier Robert Frost (Michigan State '55) and his wife Sharon were vacationing with their young daughters in New York City. Her Sigma Kappa badge and his Delta Chi badge were stolen out of a locked suitcase in their hotel room. The Frosts had no hope of recovering their loss. Thirty years later Larry Branch, a member of Kappa Alpha Order, was going through the possessions of his recently deceased father. A New York City employee, the elder Mr. Branch had collected small items off the streets, keeping them in jars at home. When sorting through the treasures, a Delta Chi badge caught young Branch's eye. After doing some research, he learned what the letters stood for and deciphered the initiation date and initials engraved on the back. With a call to headquarters, the badge soon found its way back into Sharon Frost's hands. She wrote Larry Branch with sincere gratitude. "I must say I was speechless for at least half a minute...Unfortunately my husband passed away four years ago this month...but of course the return of the pin still holds great significance for me, especially since he had 'pinned' me with it nearly 44 years ago when we were both students at Michigan State."

H. Keith McNally (Idaho '82) tells the story of a Delta Chi badge significant in his family's history. "My initiation into full membership with the Fraternity was a highly anticipated event...I was filled with pride as I was welcomed into the Bond of the Delta Chi Fraternity. All of the membership came forward to congratulate me including my cousin Tim Carper (Idaho '79). At that moment Tim called for silence as he explained to everyone that he was presenting me with a special Delta Chi membership badge." The delta was outlined in fire opals and set over a chi made of white gold. In the center of the beautiful badge, originally worn by McNally's father J. Harold McNally (Idaho '52), was a ruby. Keith had little memory of his father who had tragically died in a lumber mill fire in 1965. He poignantly recalls, "I was four years old and I remember standing on a hill overlooking the mill and watching the fire." During his University of Idaho days, the elder McNally pinned and married his wife Patricia with the badge before it was presented to his brother-in-law Delos E. "Dee" Servoss (Idaho '61). Dee pinned and married his wife Gloria before passing the badge to Tim Carper for his initiation on February 7, 1976. Tim pinned and married his wife Jodi before presenting the badge to Keith at the emotional initiation ceremony. "And yes, I pinned and married my wife, Lillian. Lill wore the badge on her wedding dress during our marriage ceremony." Keith later presented the badge to his cousin Kelly Carper (Idaho '88) who used it to pin his wife Karla. "My father's membership badge is almost magical to me. As I hold the badge in my hand the gems dance in the light. It was my father's. A man I never really knew but who I share the same bond with through the Delta Chi Fraternity. Through the badge and membership in Delta Chi I became closer to him. Likewise, I share the same bond with my only blood uncle and two cousins. The badge is a symbol of the Bond of Delta Chi for all five of us."

Senator Douglas S. Holsclaw (Arizona '25) became the third member of the Order of the White Carnation in 1977. A founder of the Arizona Chapter, Holsclaw wrote the University of Arizona fight song, "Fight Wildcats Fight" in 1930.

the new executive director, Larry P. Audlehelm (Iowa '71). Audlehelm had been active in Delta Chi since his initiation. He served as the Iowa Chapter "A", "B", "E", and rush chairman. In 1972 he was elected regent of Region IV.

Hired by M. Gary Monk (Auburn '65, "AA" 1975–77), Audlehelm brought enthusiasm and extensive knowledge of the fraternity to the position. He reported in the March 1977 *Quarterly* that Richard A. Barnes (Augusta '80) was the 40,000th brother initiated into Delta Chi. Audlehelm's efforts led to reinvigoration of alumni relations. In his first year, alumni contributions increased an impressive 60 percent. New alumni chapters were formed, and dramatic fiscal advances for the fraternity in general were recorded. Audlehelm laid out the three ways for Delta Chi to grow—expansion, every chapter pledging additional members, or merger with another fraternity. Mergers were explored and negotiations began. When word of the discussions leaked out, however, the talks ended. Audlehelm resigned during the fall of 1978 leaving Delta Chi again in need of an executive director, *Quarterly* editor, and managing director of the educational foundation.

Raymond D. Galbreth (Missouri '69) filled the executive director position in May 1979 and busily prepared to welcome delegates to Iowa City for the forty-second international convention, scheduled for August 10–12. Helping to start the Southeast Missouri Chapter, Galbreth served as its "BB" from 1976–79, was vice-regent from 1976–77, and was Region IV's regent in 1978. Much of the agenda of the 1979 convention was dedicated to establishing goals for Galbreth in his new role. Several years earlier Galbreth had responded to the *Quarterly*'s question, "Why Did You Join Delta Chi?"

In preparation for being initiated into Delta Chi over ten years ago, I was asked to write an essay entitled "Why I Want to Become a Delta Chi." Today, in trying to write what it means to be a Delta Chi, I return to the same idealistic thoughts that I talked about 10 years ago. Only now they have meaning, substance and an emotion that brings them to life. "Brotherhood," "Fraternity," "Delta Chi," "National," all mean something. What that something is, is as different as the experiences each of us have gone through. It is these experiences which give these idealistic words meaning, and as I continue to experience associating with my Fraternity and my fraternity brothers, continue to grow in depth, continue to grow in fulfillment, and I continue to grow with them. Delta Chi is my only college experience that continues to grow with me; everything (and everyone) else are just fond memories.

Galbreth has greatly impacted the growth of the fraternity and solidly remains at the helm of twenty-first-century Delta Chi.

Troy State brothers lost only one football game from 1974 to 1978. The next year, every member of the chapter traveled to the funeral of Brother Paul G. Gonzales when he tragically died in a car accident in 1979. Dorothy Gonzales wrote, "God took my wonderful son, who no one will ever replace, but in doing so he gave me a whole house of wonderful young men that I would be proud to have as my sons!"

Kansas hosted a Tom Jones party in 1979.

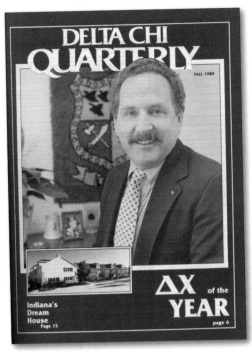

Raymond D. Galbreth (Missouri '69) became executive director of Delta Chi in 1979. He was awarded Delta Chi of the Year in 1989, between recognition of actor Kevin Costner (Fullerton '77) in 1988 and FBI Director William S. Sessions (Kansas '51) in 1990.

The 1979 Academy Award winning movie *Breaking Away* told the story of an event Indiana Delta Chis know well. The Little 500 is a fifty-mile bicycle race held annually at Indiana University in Bloomington since 1951. The Delta Chi team won the highly competitive race in 1973, 1974, 1976, 1977, 1979, 1980, 1981, and 1993. Randy Reisinger (Indiana '72) served as alumni advisor and race coach to the Delta Chis in the 1970s. Delta Chi team member Wayne Stetina rode on the 1972 and 1976 United States Olympic cycling teams. An entire year was spent preparing for the Little 500 and competition between brothers was intense for a place on the team. A checkered flag hung in the team's room asking, "What have you done

DELTA CHI FRATERNITY
42ND INTERNATIONAL CONVENTION
Iowa City, Iowa

to win the Little 500 today?" Bill Brissman (Indiana '81) and Gary Rybar (Indiana '76) served as doubles in the *Breaking Away* movie. Delta Chi Little 500 Hall of Fame members include: Eddy Van Guyse, Mark Dayton, Gary Rybar, Wayne Stetina, Bill Brissman, and Chris Gutowsky.

Although some older alumni may have frowned on longer hair and looser morals, Delta Chis were often complimented for their courtesy and helpfulness. The *Quarterly* received several letters illustrating this. A janitor at Gorham State wrote, "I have never seen any of the rules broken by the members of the Delta Chi Fraternity in the five years that they held their meetings in my building. Several times they gave me a gift to show their appreciation. They never failed to say, 'Thank you, Glen,' after a meeting. The gift which I appreciated most was that twice a group of the boys came to our Church just to show their friendship for me...I hope you will be as proud to have their Chapter as part of your

Indiana Delta Chi Wayne Stetina rode on the 1972 and 1976 United States Olympic cycling teams.

organization as I am to have their friendship." The chief of police of Valdosta, Georgia, wrote, You may not know it, but your day with us changed the opinions and attitudes around here. Most of us did not have the opportunity to attend college and some had the idea you were a bunch of spoiled rich kids just playing around. When you all came down and really went to work cleaning up in the jail when you could have been having a good time somewhere else, it showed you were concerned for your fellow man and wanted to help the less fortunate…I am not too worried about what's going to happen to this old world as long as we have fine young men like you to lead the way.

Ron Mix (Southern California '60) played his entire ten years of the AFL with the San Diego Chargers. Nicknamed the "Intellectual Assassin" for his intelligence and physical play, Mix was inducted into the Pro Football Hall of Fame in 1979. *Courtesy San Diego Chargers*

Delta Chi Quarterly

Spring/Summer 2002

Delta Chi Brothers In the Entertainment Field

"The challenges of the '80s can best be met through effectively linking the wisdom and maturity of our alumni to the optimism and vibrancy of our undergraduates."

RAYMOND F. BORELLI (ILLINOIS '58, "AA" 1981–85)

Illinois initiated five brothers of the Lyons family into the bond. The brotherly brothers are, from left to right, Robert '85, Thomas '83, Joseph '89, Mark '84, and Richard '79.

Charles Marshall (Illinois '51) spent his career working for Bell Systems and AT&T. Marshall was vice chairman of AT&T when he retired in 1989 and was Delta Chi of the Year in 1993.

The decade began with a celebration of Delta Chi's ninetieth anniversary. Robert P. LaBouy (Washington '66, "AA" 1979–81) spoke of the impending centennial, "We must also keep in mind our next hundred years. There are many challenges facing Delta Chi… Yesterday's memories were great…let's make tomorrow's memories strong, enduring and the best in our history." Through the *Quarterly*, Ray Galbreth hoped to share the intricacies of Delta Chi history by featuring pivotal issues such as single membership. History shared the headline with current issues such as fraternity liquor liability. Some issues remained consistent through the years. As they had in 1929, convention delegates in 1980 addressed hazing. The fraternity officers wrote, "It is the feeling of the Officers and staff of the General Fraternity that hazing has greatly declined within Delta Chi in the past five years. Through this new program we hope to continue that progress and reaffirm the historic stance our brothers took over 50 years ago."

Delta Chis helped shaped the decade by leading exploration into new frontiers of technology and science. An article in the Fall 1980 *Quarterly* by the former vice president and treasurer of AT&T, Charles Marshall (Illinois '51) prophesied much of what was to come, "A few years from now, you may turn on your home computer terminal to visit the library. When you're away from home, you'll be able to receive phone calls in your car. And you'll get useful information from a talking computer." Marshall was later appointed executive vice president of AT&T and was in charge of "Baby Bell," the name used to refer to the Bell subsidiary that handled operations in unregulated areas such as data processing. Marshall was named vice chairman of the board of AT&T in 1985 and held this position until his retirement in 1989. Another Delta Chi explored the depths of the ocean. Mel Fisher (Purdue '45) spent decades searching for the 1622 wreck of the *Atocha* off the Florida Keys. Despite the optimistic motto of "Today's the Day," Fisher was plagued with financial difficulties and personal tragedy during his quest, including the death of his son. On July 20, 1985, he discovered the wreck and its estimated $450 million cache. The riches of the *Atocha*, including forty tons of gold and silver, continue to be excavated today despite Fisher's death in 1998. Fisher was Delta Chi of the Year in 1994.

Delta Chi literally crossed the boundaries of a new frontier when on June 27, 1982, astronaut Henry W. "Hank" Hartsfield Jr. (Auburn '54) took his fraternity pin into space. A NASA astronaut since 1969, Hartsfield piloted his flight of the *Columbia* twenty years before the shuttle's disaster on its twenty-eighth mission. Hartsfield's mission, called STS-4, was the fourth shuttle mission overall. Orbiting Earth 113 times over the course of a week, Hartsfield and Commander Thomas K. Mattingly were the first to land the shuttle on a concrete runway. Hartsfield served as "B" of his Auburn Chapter while an undergraduate. "What I remember most was the fellowship we shared. Living,

"The World's Greatest Treasure Hunter," Mel Fisher (Purdue '45), welcomed Oklahoma brothers Douglas Amyx, left, and Jeff Kelley, right, to his Treasure Salvors' Museum in Key West.

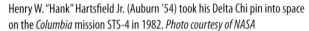

Henry W. "Hank" Hartsfield Jr. (Auburn '54) took his Delta Chi pin into space on the *Columbia* mission STS-4 in 1982. *Photo courtesy of NASA*

Orbiting for 7 days, 1 hour, 9 minutes, and 31 seconds, STS-4 landed on July 4 at Edwards Air Force Base in California where they were met by President and Mrs. Reagan. Reagan remarked to Hartsfield, "You've given the American people a Fourth of July to remember…and this has gotta' beat firecrackers!" *Photo courtesy of NASA*

working and playing together just made life better." The NASA tradition of waking the astronauts with meaningful music continued on this mission. The flight log shows on day four a taped message was played for Hartsfield, as it was his wedding anniversary; day five began with the theme from *Chariots of Fire*; and on day six Hartsfield was awakened by Delta Chi Fraternity songs.

In the late 1970s many began to believe the fraternity's existing system of governance was flawed and ill-designed to support continued growth. After the 1979 convention a task force was formed, the governance committee. After several years of research and analysis their

"position paper" was presented at the 1981 convention. They determined that the board of regents was undemocratic and cumbersome. There were simply too many chapters and colonies for any one regent to handle. Few regents felt they were adequately fulfilling both their roles of executive board member and undergraduate liaison. The governance committee, led by Greg Hauser (Michigan State '75) and Monte Johnson (Ohio State '69), completed their final proposal and presented it, endorsed by the Delta Chi Board of Regents, at the 1983 convention held in Nashville. The new board was to have seven members, all elected at staggered conventions, to serve four-year terms. The regions' sizes and numbers would be flexible.

Every two years the chapters and colonies would be equally apportioned into regions. The complete report filled twenty detailed pages and was available upon request from headquarters. The recommendation was not approved at the 1983 convention. The current form of government remained unchanged except chapters were given weighted voting based on their size.

After thirty years in existence, a full-time employee was sought to head the Delta Chi Educational Foundation fundraising efforts. John F. Caperton Jr. (SMU '49) assumed the duties of foundation managing director in 1982 and set goals to build a significant endowment. In honor of alumni contributions to society in general, the first Delta Chi of the Year award was given at the 1983 convention. To be eligible for the award, a nominee must have distinguished himself in such a manner as to be recognized by their peers throughout the land. The first recipient was Senator Henry M. "Scoop" Jackson (Washington '34). It was clear Delta Chi meant a great deal to Jackson. He wrote, "There were thirteen pledges, including myself in 1930… The friendships we made were the most durable of my life and I still keep in touch with several of my fraternity brothers." In 1984 the second Delta Chi of the Year award was presented to astronaut Henry W. Hartsfield, Jr.

As delegates prepared for the 1985 convention in Chicago grand milestones were approaching. The fraternity would soon initiate its 50,000th member and its assets approached the million-dollar level. The 50,000th initiate was Dave Granger (Iowa '88). Ray Galbreth presented

House clean up at Alabama.

Dr. Marsh White (Penn State faculty, Order of the White Carnation) attended the Penn State annual retreat in the summer of 1983.

Lawrence R. Herkimer (SMU '48) is the grandfather of modern cheerleading. A SMU yell leader in the 1940s, Herkimer founded the National Cheerleader Association in 1948, originated a jump called the Herkie, patented hidden handle pompoms, and ran cheer camps attended by tens of thousands. Founding the company with $600, he sold his empire in 1986 for $20 million.

In 1984 Southwestern College in Memphis, Tennessee, was renamed Rhodes College in honor of Dr. Peyton N. Rhodes (Virginia '20).

DELTA CHI
LSU - FSU Party
September 10, 1983

The Lehigh brothers won the intramural weightlifting championship eight years in a row during the 1980s. In 1985 they proudly posed with some of their many trophies in front of their house at 233 West Packer.

Granger with a jeweled badge and his shingle mounted on a plaque. Brother Ed Graziore, who was initiate number 50,001, said he was very happy for Granger, but he wished it had been him. On October 14, 1985, the first Henry M. "Scoop" Jackson Leadership College was held with the purpose of developing the leadership skills of undergraduates. The 1985 Delta Chi of the Year was Dr. Peyton Nalle Rhodes (Virginia '20). Dr. Rhodes received the honor posthumously, as he passed away in November 1984. Rhodes was a physics professor at Southwestern College in Memphis and was the president of the institution for sixteen years. Rhodes was humbled when the Southwestern board of trustees changed the school's name to Rhodes College honoring his half-century of dedicated service.

Dram shop laws came into effect in 1988 and liability became a buzzword. Drinking ages were raised and chapters were told they could no longer purchase alcohol with chapter funds. With only two years remaining until the centennial convention in Ithaca, five new colonies were established in 1988 and seven chapters were chartered. With such a significant milestone on the horizon Larry P. Audlehelm (Iowa '71, "AA" 1987–90) wrote, "We do not know fully what we do, so let us do good. Let us do good for the sake of our brothers, not yet met who will carry the banner into the coming century. Let us do good for the strength of the Bond. Let us do good for the love of Delta Chi. And, by so doing it can truly be said we have served the Founding and the future well."

From left to right, John M. Shelby (Sacramento '86), Gregory F. Hauser (Michigan State '75), Otis R. Bowen (Indiana '39), and James V. Ferrara (Michigan State '81) posed in 1986. Bowen, governor of Indiana from 1973 to 1981 and secretary of health and human services from 1985 to 1989, was receiving the Delta Chi of the Year award.

This photo of Christopher Ashton Kutcher (Iowa) was in the Spring/Summer 2002 *Delta Chi Quarterly*. Kutcher is a recognizable Delta Chi face.

DELTA CHI
White Carnation
March 7, 1987

Georgia Southern brothers readied their float for the 1988 homecoming parade.

The Indiana Chapter was excited about the major addition being planned to 1100 North Jordan.

MARGE LEE: DELTA CHI'S FIRST LADY EMERITUS

IN THE FALL OF 1989 THE *QUARTERLY* RAN A TRIBUTE TO MARGE LEE.

HIRED AS A "PART-TIME" WORKER TO HELP OUT AN ALUMNI DUES MAILING IN SEPTEMBER OF 1964 BY EXECUTIVE SECRETARY HAROLD "BUC" BUCHANAN, WISCONSIN '35, MARGE LEE HAS BEEN WITH DELTA CHI FOR 25 YEARS. SHE HAS BEEN THE "DELTA CHI MOM" FOR NUMEROUS FIELDMEN AND THE PERSON BEHIND THE SCENES THAT HAS KEPT THE HEADQUARTERS FUNCTIONING. WHILE KNOWN TO THOUSANDS BY NAME AND HER FRIENDLY VOICE ON THE PHONE, ONLY THOSE CLOSE TO THE OPERATIONS OF THE HEADQUARTERS REALIZE THE DEBT DELTA CHI OWES THIS SPECIAL PERSON. DOING THE WORK OF TWO PEOPLE IS "AN AVERAGE" WORKLOAD FOR MARGE. FOR OVER TEN YEARS SHE HAS KEPT NOT ONLY THE MEMBERSHIP RECORD OF THE FRATERNITY BUT THE FINANCIAL RECORDS AS WELL. INVENTORY CONTROL, STAFF TRAINING, ORDER FILLING AND WORKFLOW MANAGEMENT ARE JUST "PART OF THE JOB." EXECUTIVE DIRECTOR GALBRETH STATES, "IN THE TEN YEARS THAT I HAVE BEEN EXECUTIVE DIRECTOR I HAVE NEVER ONCE WORRIED ABOUT WHETHER MARGE'S JOB IS BEING DONE OR BEING DONE RIGHT. ONLY AN OFFICE ADMINISTRATOR CAN KNOW THE TRUE VALUE OF THAT STATEMENT." SINCE THERE ARE NO WORDS TO PROPERLY EXPRESS OUR FEELINGS FOR MARGE AND OUR GRATITUDE FOR HER HARD WORK AND UNTIRING DEVOTION, THE *QUARTERLY* SIMPLY STANDS IN SILENT RESPECT FOR AND DEEP APPRECIATION OF A VERY SPECIAL PERSON AND HER 25 YEARS OF DEVOTION TO DELTA CHI FRATERNITY.

IN HER THIRTY-EIGHTH YEAR OF DELTA CHI SERVICE, AT THE 2002 CONVENTION MARGE LEE WAS DECREED DELTA CHI'S FIRST LADY EMERITUS. AT THE 2004 CONVENTION THE OUTSTANDING "C" AWARD WAS RENAMED THE MARGE LEE "C" AWARD. IN 2007, AFTER HAVING MAJOR BACK SURGERY MARGE WAS OUT OF THE OFFICE FOR A BRIEF TIME. SHE RALLIED, HOWEVER, AND ATTENDED THE LAS VEGAS CONVENTION IN 2008. SADLY, A MONTH LATER, FORTY-FOUR YEARS AFTER JOINING DELTA CHI'S STAFF, MARGE PASSED AWAY. HER FAMILY WROTE, "...IT IS OBVIOUS WHY SHE WAS SO PROUD OF HER BOYS, AND WE UNDERSTAND A LITTLE BETTER WHAT SHE MEANT TO ALL OF HER DELTA CHI FAMILY. WE ARE TRULY HONORED TO HAVE SHARED HER WITH YOU FOR ALL THESE YEARS." THE *QUARTERLY* SIMPLY SAID, "SHE WAS MORE DEDICATED TO DELTA CHI THAN WE DESERVED, AND WE WERE TRULY BLESSED TO HAVE HER."

CHAPTER ELEVEN

1990–1999

The Delta Chi Fraternity Centennial Convention
Ithaca & Syracuse, NY ~ August 8-12, 1990

Brothers at the 1990 centennial convention gathered outside of Ithaca at Founder Monroe Sweetland's grave. They are, from left to right, Rob Chapin (Appalachian State '85), Glenn Weiss (LSU '84), Larry P. Audlehelm (Iowa '71), Jeff Albright (Chico '87), Mike Carroll (Auburn '71), Anthony Hipp (Appalachian State '87), and David Surber (Colorado '83).

"Delta Chi is my only college experience that continues to grow with me; everything, and everyone, else are just fond memories."

RAY GALBRETH (MISSOURI '69)
EXECUTIVE DIRECTOR SINCE 1979

From left to right at the centennial convention were Larry Audlehelm, Greg Hauser, Cindy Costner, Kevin Costner, and Mike Carroll.

Close to five hundred brothers gathered for the 1990 centennial convention, the largest gathering in Delta Chi history up to that point. Ten full-sized buses carried delegates from Syracuse to Ithaca and Cornell University for the day. Many brothers stopped to visit the grave of Founder Monroe Marsh Sweetland where Larry Audlehelm (Iowa '71) and Mike Carroll (Auburn '71) held an informal memorial and placed a wreath. The fraternity began its second century with 120 chapters and colonies on the roll. As he had in 1987, Kevin Costner (Fullerton '77) spoke at the 1990 convention, "When I meet you, and when I look into your eyes, and when I shake your hand, I feel a friendship. I know that you talk to other people about me and when you do I feel your support. As a result of our association, there's a bond between us."

Fifty brothers attended the sixth "Scoop" Jackson Leadership College, held in Iowa City in August of 1991. Joseph J. DeFazio II (Fredonia Colony) expressed the opinion of many when he wrote, "Keeping the college in Iowa City would be a wise move in my opinion as it would give more brothers the opportunity to attend and lead to a great diversity of brothers and chapters in attendance." Five hundred members and guests met in Irvine, California, for the forty-eighth Delta Chi convention in 1992. Joseph Lacchia (NYU '25) shared the tradition of the handshake across

The sixth Senator Henry M. "Scoop" Jackson Leadership College was held in Iowa City in 1991.

"I SAW MY DUTY AND I DID IT."
DR. MARSH W. WHITE

ON APRIL 22, 1996, BROTHER MARSH W. WHITE (PENN STATE FACULTY) CELEBRATED HIS ONE-HUNDREDTH BIRTHDAY IN THE COMPANY OF FELLOW DELTA CHIS. WHITE SERVED AS "AA" FROM 1952 TO 1954, "CC" FROM 1940 TO 1954, AND "DD" FROM 1935 TO 1940. HE IS AN "AA" EMERITUS, MEMBER OF THE ORDER OF THE WHITE CARNATION, AND HAD A LONG HISTORY OF SERVICE TO THE DELTA CHI EDUCATIONAL FOUNDATION. HE WAS THE FOUNDATION'S EDUCATIONAL ADVISOR FROM 1965 UNTIL 1988 AND WAS SERVING ON ITS BOARD OF DIRECTORS WHEN HE TURNED ONE HUNDRED. WHITE DESIGNED THE PLEDGE PIN, THE PLEDGE CEREMONY, AND IN 1937, ORGANIZED THE FIRST REGIONAL CONFERENCE. "I WAS DELIGHTED THAT SOMETHING I ORGANIZED TURNED OUT TO BE SO SUCCESSFUL."

ALTHOUGH UNABLE TO ATTEND THE CENTENNIAL CONVENTION IN 1990, WHITE SPOKE TO THE DELEGATES BY SPEAKERPHONE. THEY IN TURN UNANIMOUSLY RESOLVED TO MARK HIM AS OFFICIALLY IN ATTENDANCE. BROTHER WHITE TOLD OF HIS ATTENDANCE AT TWENTY-THREE CONVENTIONS, A DELTA CHI RECORD. "I HAVE BEEN TO EVERY ONE SINCE 1929. THEY ALWAYS START THE SAME WAY. AT THE OPENING SESSION, THE PRESIDING OFFICER SAYS, 'EVERYBODY PLEASE STAND.' THEN HE ASKS, 'IS THIS YOUR FIRST DELTA CHI CONVENTION? IF SO, PLEASE SIT DOWN.' AND AN ENORMOUS NUMBER OF PEOPLE SIT. THEN HIS SAYS, 'IF THIS IS YOUR SECOND CONVENTION, PLEASE SIT.' AND SO ON THROUGH THIRD, FOURTH, FIFTH, TENTH, FIFTEENTH, TWENTIETH, ETC. SOON I AM THE ONLY PERSON LEFT STANDING. IT HAS BEEN THAT WAY FOR SEVERAL CONVENTIONS NOW. I GET A BIG HAND."

BROTHER WHITE PASSED AWAY ON JANUARY 23, 1999.

Gary H. Mears (Iowa '58) was promoted to lieutenant general at a special Pentagon ceremony in August 1991. General Colin L. Powell, chairman of the Joint Chiefs of Staff, pinned on Lieutenant General Mears's third star with the assistance of Mears's wife Jackie.

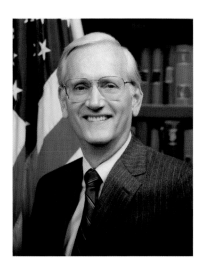

The decade's first Delta Chi of the Year was William S. "Bill" Sessions (Kansas '51), director of the Federal Bureau of Investigation from 1987 until 1993. He coined the phrase, "Winners don't use drugs."

The Kansas Chapter house was proudly rededicated in 2000.

the centuries with the delegates. Present at the 1940 convention, Lacchia listened to Founder Sweetland address his brothers. He then joined the line to shake Sweetland's hand. Lacchia started a handshake at the 1992 gathering that made its way around the room. This poignant gesture insured that the Delta Chis of the 1990s, including his son Joseph F. Lacchia Jr. (Michigan State '63) were connected to the fraternity's roots.

A positive vote to increase chapter and colony dues and the focus on expansion led to Delta Chi's office staff reaching its highest historical numbers in the 1990s. Headquarters needed expansion and remodeling to handle the larger staff and workload. The board of regents considered relocating the office but ultimately decided to stay in Iowa City and 314 Church Street received a new addition in 1993. Risk management was the largest issue now facing

Mankato State brothers posed in the 1990s.

the fraternity. Strong stances were taken requiring chapters to follow Delta Chi's Risk Management Policy (FIPG) and the hazing statutes. The board of regents adopted a zero tolerance policy on hazing and, for the good of the fraternity, several chapters were placed on probation. Great changes in behavior were expected in the chapters.

Two new ceremonies were put into place in the mid-1990s. In 1992 the Alumni Ceremony was written in an attempt to combat the "I Was a Delta Chi" syndrome. Held to mark the transition from student member to alumnus, the ceremony was designed to remind brothers of their Delta Chi bond and officially welcome them to the ranks of alumni. Nearly 150 alumni quickly jumped at the chance to participate in this new ceremony. A non-secret Memorial Ceremony was also designed, intended to be held at a brother's graveside. The John J. Kuhn Award for Service to the Fraternity Movement was initiated in 1992. This award was designed by the Delta Chi Board of Regents to recognize individuals who have dedicated their lives to the betterment of the fraternity community. The first recipient reflected Delta Chi's concern about member safety. Retiring "AA" Greg

Regional conferences continued to play an important role in the fraternity.

Minnesota and Michigan both celebrated their centennials in 1992 with gatherings of alumni from six decades.

Indiana Brothers Neil Stoeckel, Todd Hancock, Jeff Allman, Scott Hallberg, and Steve Hoeferle (pictured from left to right) carried on the chapter's long history of Little 500 championships in 1993.

Thomas W. Glasgow (Michigan State '68), shown here with his wife Linda, was named executive vice president and chief operations officer of McDonald's Corporation in 1991. He was given the Delta Chi of the Year award in 1995.

Hauser (Michigan State '75) present the Kuhn Award to Eileen Stevens, founder of CHUCK (Committee to Halt Useless College Killings). Stevens's son Chuck was killed during an alcohol-related hazing incident. She worked nationally with college students and fraternities to prevent hazing and was greatly deserving of the Kuhn Award.

Four decades after its founding, the Delta Chi Educational Foundation was due for strategic assessment. A volunteer committee gathered to evaluate the foundation and determine its mission going forward. Members included Keith Shriver (Florida '79), Fred Hammert (Oklahoma '60), John "Pete" Copeland (Indiana '49), Frank Voris (Illinois '61), Andrew Smith (Georgia Tech '94), M. Gary Monk (Auburn '65), Raymond Galbreth (Missouri '69), Boyd Boehlje (Iowa State '61), Paul Bohlman (Ohio State '70), Larry Audlehelm (Iowa '71), Jimmie "Doc" Underwood (Kansas '51), and Michael Carroll (Auburn '71). The new mission statement for the foundation read, "Our mission is to challenge our brotherhood to a lifelong commitment to the improvement of our world by developing the leaders of the future."

With continued emphasis on alumni relations, Steven P. Bossart (Kent State '90) was named director of alumni services. Keeping pace with technology, and hoping to encourage alumni communication, the Winter-Spring 1994–95 *Quarterly* announced Delta Chi could be found "on the information superhighway." Emails flew in preparation for the fiftieth international convention. Nearly four hundred alumni gathered in Dallas for this 1996 event. George Obear (DePauw '28) shared Sweetland's handshake across the centuries with delegates. The convention honoree was Jefferson Coleman (Alabama '29) who was "A" of his chapter, served as "CC" from 1952 to 1954, as "AA"

M. Gary Monk (Auburn '65) and Patti Carroll, wife of Mike Carroll, enjoyed a convention gathering.

from 1954 to 1956, is "AA" emeritus, and is a member of the Order of the White Carnation. Greg Hauser (Michigan State '75) joined Coleman as a member of the Order of the White Carnation. Hauser was also awarded the highest honor from the Fraternity Executives Association in 1996, the Distinguished Service Award, recognizing his outstanding service to the entire fraternity movement.

The men of Frostburg Colony illustrated their Delta Chi spirit.

As the 1990s drew to a close, Delta Chi was proud to have seven alumni serving on Capitol Hill. The 105th Congress included Senator Richard C. Shelby (Alabama '57), Senator Craig Thomas (Wyoming alumnus), Senator Larry Craig (Idaho '67), Representative Sam Johnson (SMU '51), Representative John L. Mica (Florida '67), Representative Dan Miller (Florida '64), and Representative Bob Stump (Arizona State '51). Representative Johnson was the 1998 Delta Chi of the Year. Another Delta Chi long on the political stage, four-time governor of Alabama George Wallace (Alabama '42), passed away in 1998.

William A. "Bill" Williams (Gannon '83, "AA" 1998–2002) frankly wrote about acceptance in the Fall/Winter 1998 *Quarterly*. "The 51st Convention elected me to the position of 'AA.' This marks the first time that an African-American has been elected to this position in the history of the Fraternity. This milestone in

HANDS ACROSS THE CENTURIES

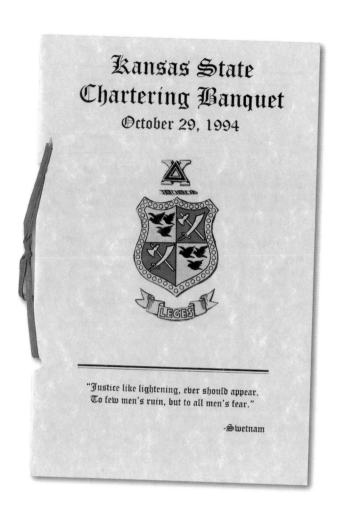

The 1994 convention was held in Atlanta.

Delta Chi history takes on a greater sense of achievement when one stops to consider that, until the 1954 Convention, membership in Delta Chi was restricted to white male college or university students. I thank you for seeing beyond the color and into the content of my heart and the character of my spirit." Upon Williams's election, Delta Chi became the first traditionally white fraternity to have an African American as its president. The ceremonial badge and neck ribbon, usually worn by the wife of the "AA" elect, was presented by the unmarried Bill Williams to lifetime Delta Chi sweetheart and heart of the headquarters, Marge Lee. Williams was reelected to his second term as "AA" at the 2002 convention.

At the 1998 convention, the last of the century, Delta Chi officially closed eight chapters. Three were closed due to risk management violations. The remaining five languished due to loss in membership. Fraternity leadership, however, remained hopeful that if all adhered to the basic values of Delta Chi, they would prosper. As the millennium approached the fraternity

recognized its fifth member of the New Founder donor category. These are men whose generosity to the Delta Chi Fraternity or Foundation exceeds $100,000. F. Phil Yang (Abracadabra '80 and founding father of his chapter) joined only four other brothers in this distinguished category: Bernhard C. Shaffer (Penn State '25), Clayton T. Roberts (Florida '31), Gene A. Johnson (Oklahoma State '58), and Fredrick B. Hammert (Oklahoma '60). Generosity such as this buoyed Delta Chi confidently into the twenty-first century.

Mrs. Robert S. (Catherine) Justice donated this badge, believed to be the oldest in existence at the time, to the fraternity in 1994. Willard Fitzer (Michigan 1892), the original owner and a founder of the Michigan Chapter, gave the badge to his young neighbor, Robert Justice (DePauw '33), in 1930. Justice gave the pin to Catherine in 1941 as an engagement present.

The Whitewater Chapter won best homecoming float with their dragon in 1994.

The 1996 convention met in Dallas, Texas.

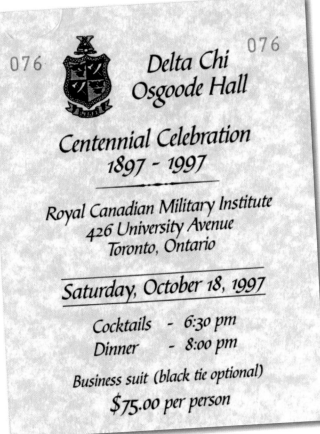

Convention Program

The Delta Chi Fraternity

International Convention

ST LOUIS

August 5 thru 9, 1998

...believing that great advantages are to be derived...

Scott Curcio (Northwestern 2000) was the 1999 homecoming king.

Three former "AAs", Mike Carroll (Auburn '71), Bill Williams (Gannon '83), and Greg Hauser (Michigan State '75), were at the Penn State Chapter in January 1999 for Marsh White's memorial service.

This 1999 group of Southern California brothers illustrates the diversity of Delta Chi.

Chapter Twelve:
2000–2010

The Summer/Fall 2000 *Quarterly* cover featured Delta Chi's All-Time Football Team members including Pro Football Hall of Famers Ron Mix (Southern California '60) and Leo Nomellini (Minnesota '50).

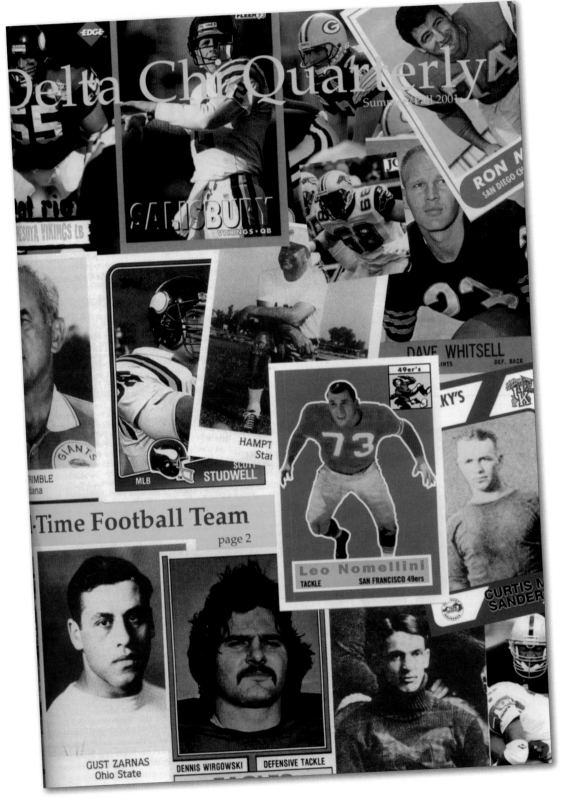

"The Ship of State may shattered be, The stars fall from the sky, The mighty oak, a fallen tree, But, ever Delta Chi."

"THE SONS OF DELTA CHI"
DELTA CHI SONGS 1912

Marge Lee posed in 2002 with one of her favorite former staff members, United States Congressman John L. Mica (Florida '67).

The new century began with the fifty-second convention, held in August of 2000 at Squaw Peak in Phoenix, Arizona. George Obear (DePauw '30) tied the late Marsh White with a record number of twenty-three conventions attended. The *Quarterly* continued to connect brothers of the present to brothers of the past. Issues focused on members of note in various fields: baseball, sports, government, and entertainment. The individual luminaries, however, were only a small part of the fabric of Delta Chi. Chapter officers, fraternity officers, volunteers, and the people behind the scenes continued to be the strength of the organization. Marge Lee began her thirty-seventh year in the office and Ray Galbreth, his twenty-second year as executive director. Charles A. Mancuso (Florida State '84, "AA" 2002–04) wrote, "We as Delta Chis are part of a greater picture. Individuals are part of a community and for us that projects from the Chapter level through the University level through our International Fraternity and into society as a whole."

A highlight of the 2002 Orlando convention was an address by Judy Griffin, grand-niece of Founder Peter Schermerhorn Johnson. Griffin shared family stories and presented the fraternity with Johnson's badge. The badge has stones around the delta with a peridot center. This was the first founder's badge to be included in the fraternity's archives and was unanimously recognized as a Delta Chi treasure. Congressman John L. Mica (Florida '67) gave an inspirational keynote address and George Obear, at what would be his last convention, began the meaningful handshake across the centuries. The life of the fraternity continued to be recorded by the *Quarterly*, whose one-hundredth birthday was in 2003. Through eighteen different editors and a variety of sizes and shapes, the *Quarterly* has kept Delta Chis connected for a century. The first edition of the *Quarterly*, printed in 1903, was sent to the fourteen active chapters, 250 undergraduate members, and a handful of alumni. In a concrete testament to the fraternity's growth, 60,000 copies of the fall 2003 edition were printed and mailed.

As they had for a century, brothers encountered each other around the world while serving in military or charitable endeavors. Recognizing each other through Delta Chi t-shirts, Josh Wentz (Truman State '00) and Justin Ramirez (Long Beach '02) met in the Republic of Bulgaria while training with the United States Peace Corps. Brothers Alan Hargreaves, while serving in the US Air Force, and Fred Weixeldorfer, while serving in the US Army, took time to pose in Iraq with the American flag and a Delta Chi handshake in 2003. J. Philip Ludvigson (American '96) and Fred Minnick (Oklahoma State '01) served together in Iraq. Ludvigson wrote, "Delta Chi brothers have fought and made the ultimate sacrifice in every U.S. war for over a century. We are proud to continue that history of dedication to the ideals of our nation and our fraternity. I guess you could say that this is the ultimate philanthropy project." Through the service and dedication of

Bill Williams (Gannon '83, "AA" 1998–2002) and Executive Director Ray Galbreth posed with Judy Griffin, grand-niece of Founder Peter Schermerhorn Johnson, at the 2002 convention.

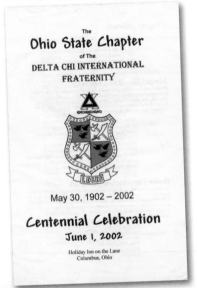

Brothers in Iraq were Fred Minnick (Oklahoma State '01) and J. Philip Ludvigson (American '96).

HANDS ACROSS THE CENTURIES

Delta Chi 2003
Staff Reunion
Iowa City, Iowa

314 Church Street

thousands of brothers, the handshake of Delta Chi has not only circled the globe, it has had a positive influence wherever it has traveled.

Social functions continued to play a large role in the Delta Chi college experience. The brothers in Idaho continued their chapter's annual Pirate Dance tradition in 2004. For the sixty-ninth year, they roasted a pig and spent days turning their house into a pirates' paradise. A large rope-bridge was built from the sidewalk, over a moat, and to the front door. Their brothers who conceived of the party in 1935 would surely have enjoyed the event.

In a gathering gone terribly wrong, Steven Judd (New Mexico State '06) lost his life. The

Gil Werntz (former "A" and then "BB" for Georgia Southern '85) and his son Gil posed with Dr. Jimmie J. "Doc" Underwood (Kansas '51) at the 2004 Orlando convention. Werntz was a Delta Chi Chapter Luminary in 1985 and won the Meritorious Service Award in 2007.

The George Tech Chapter prepared for homecoming in 2001 with Philanthropy Day (above) and posed in 2004 during the annual Greek Week tug of war (below).

The UNLV brothers were the 2004 intramural sports Rebel Cup Champions.

Delta Chi 54th International Convention
August 4-8, 2004   Washington, D.C.

Winter/Spring 2005 *Quarterly* told Judd's story in an attempt to prevent future tragedies. Recently elected "A" of his chapter, a small group of friends and some brothers took Judd out to celebrate his twenty-first birthday. The unfortunately common practice of celebrating twenty-one years with extreme intoxication resulted in Judd's death. His father, Steve Judd, expressed intense pain of this experience in a letter written to the *Quarterly*. "When you pass on that last drink of the night, remember our son and your brother Steven Judd. Hopefully, no other Delta Chi chapters will have to endure the guilt and suffering that the NMSU chapter will have to endure forever."

Despite continued attempts to educate members, eight chapters were on corrective action for alcohol violations of the risk management policy in 2005. Upon the occasion of the Florida Chapter returning to campus in 2007, Congressman John L. Mica (Florida '67), 2005 Delta Chi of the Year, reminded his brothers, "The image of Delta Chi and other fraternities will always be a reflection of the conduct of their individual members…it is my hope that every undergraduate and alumnus

2005 DELTA CHI LEADERSHIP COLLEGE
JULY 22-24, 2005

member will remember how important their individual actions will be to both the reputation and future of Delta Chi."

Six new chapters were on the roster in 2005: Georgia Southern, Illinois State, Pittsburgh, William and Mary, West Georgia, and Rhode Island. With the last Senator Henry M. Jackson Leadership College held in 2001, the Delta Chi Board of Regents felt the fraternity needed to step in and fill that educational void. The first leadership college attendees explored the state of the fraternity and made personal commitments to live Delta Chi's values in 2005. Raymond Galbreth reminded the group that "Delta Chi's value is under re-evaluation each and every day." The first "A"s' Academy was held in January 2006 as the newest edition to the leadership curriculum. Represented were 113 of Delta Chi's 121 chapters. Collectively the group established the goal of making the 2006 Cleveland convention the largest gathering of Delta Chis in history. In a quiet, private moment in 2005 one Delta Chi was reminded of the impact the fraternity had on his life. On one of his last visits before her death, James English (WMU '89) told his mother he had recently attended a regional Delta Chi conference. She shared her belief that the pledging and his subsequent initiation into Delta Chi "resulted in an amazing

The 2006 Delta Chi of the Year, James B. Stewart (DePauw '73), won the Pulitzer Prize for explanatory journalism in 1987. He is the author of best sellers *Den of Thieves, Blood Sport, Heart of a Soldier,* and *DisneyWar*.

The beautiful Alabama Chapter house was originally built in 1971 with a wing added in the mid-1980s. More expansion is planned to begin in 2013.

transformation and maturing of her youngest child…My mother was sold on the value of my pledging Delta Chi nearly twenty years ago and thought enough to share it with me in the twilight of her life."

The goal of creating the largest Delta Chi gathering up to that point was achieved in 2006 as three hundred student members and more than two hundred alumni gathered in Cleveland. For local flavor brothers attended a Cleveland Indians game and watched "AA" Steve Bossart (Kent State '90) throw out the first pitch of the game. Along with breaking convention attendance records, an historic step was taken at the 2006 convention when Bossart announced an official fraternity philanthropy partnership. Aligning with the V Foundation for Cancer Research, Delta Chi brothers around the world would now be focused on a

At the 2006 convention, Steven P. Bossart (Kent State '90, "AA" 2004–08) threw out the first pitch for a Cleveland Indians' game.

Delta Chis showed their patriotism in the Cleveland stands and cheered wildly when "AA" Bossart took the field.

red buff & green

delta chi – environmentally conscious

Delta Chi joined the green conversation in 2007 by asking chapters to assess their houses' environmental impact.

Ben Pakulski (Western Ontario '04) was a founding member of his Delta Chi chapter. With arms measuring twenty-one inches, Pakulski won first place at the Canadian Bodybuilding Federation Championships in 2008 and second in both the 2007 and 2008 North American Bodybuilding Championships.
Photo by Garry Bartlett

DELTA CHI
56TH INTERNATIONAL CONVENTION 2008
LAS VEGAS, NEVADA

single cause and organization. Collectively the fraternity committed to raising $100,000 by the 2008 convention, and a check was presented to the foundation for $101,963 during the opening events of the Las Vegas gathering. The foundation named a 2008 V Foundation Scholar Grant in the fraternity's name. The Delta Chi Scholar Grant was awarded to Sendurai Mani, PhD, in hopes of furthering his cancer research at the University of Texas M.D. Anderson Cancer Center. A second project was named in recognition of Delta Chi's contributions in 2010 and the fraternity is well on its way to a third sponsorship.

On December 7, 2009, the 100,000th Delta Chi brother was initiated. A duplicate shingle of Kurtis Driehuizen (Connecticut '14) hangs at headquarters to commemorate this significant fraternity milestone. At the time of Driehuizen's initiation, there were over 190 Delta Chi brothers serving their country at war. Raymond

Three "AAs" got into the spirit of the 2008 Las Vegas convention. Blue Elvis is Thomas S. Horowitz (Michigan State '87), white Elvis is Steven P. Bossart (Kent State '90), and red Elvis is Ratheen C. Damle (Texas '01). They posed with dedicated V Foundation fundraisers from South Dakota State, Ben Wise ('08, former "A") and Troy Miller ('07).

The December 12, 2009, wedding of Ash and Ratheen C. Damle (Texas '01, "DD" 2008–10) served as a Delta Chi reunion. Behind the couple, from left to right, are Trent Unterbrink (Tri-State '98), Thomas Horowitz (Michigan State '87, "AA" 2008–10), Eric Kerstetter (Auburn '00), Miles Washburn (Massachusetts '85, "CC" 2008–10), Jeff McAdoo (New Mexico State '01), Eric Baer (Texas '02), and A. D. Damle (Texas '07). Attending the event, but not pictured, were Jason Rodriguez (Texas '03) and David Tumbry (Texas '03).

F. Borelli (Illinois '58, "AA" emeritus) diligently attempted to keep track of all serving brothers and report their names to the *Quarterly* for recognition. "Delta Chis at War–We Salute You" became a regular *Quarterly* feature.

While many served abroad, brothers at home continued to focus on philanthropy. A check for $130,000 was presented to the V Foundation at the 2010 New Orleans convention. Dr. Jimmie J. "Doc" Underwood (Kansas '51, "BB" emeritus), president of the Delta Chi Educational Foundation 1983–92 and member of the Order of the White Carnation, began the handshake across the centuries at the conclusion of the New Orleans gathering. Tying George Obear with attendance at twenty-three conventions, in August of 2012 "Doc" plans to attend his twenty-fourth convention in Pittsburgh. Underwood poignantly wrote in his Delta Chi recollections, "Now I am the only one left…"

CANOEING FOR CHARITY

IN 1932 ALBERT S. TOUSLEY (MINNESOTA '24) NAVIGATED THE LENGTH OF THE MISSISSIPPI RIVER IN A SEVENTEEN-FOOT CANOE. THE ARDUOUS TRIP TOOK TOUSLEY THREE MONTHS AND HAD NOT BEEN SUCCESSFULLY COMPLETED SINCE 1881. TOUSLEY WOULD HAVE ENJOYED WATCHING SOUTH DAKOTA STATE BROTHERS BEN WISE ('08) AND MARK YORK ('12) CARRY THEIR CANOE INTO THE 2010 NEW ORLEANS MARRIOTT WHERE 185 DELTA CHIS GATHERED FOR THE FIFTY-SEVENTH INTERNATIONAL CONVENTION. BEGINNING AT BROOKINGS, SOUTH DAKOTA, THE MEN ARRIVED IN NEW ORLEANS AFTER FORTY-EIGHT DAYS, JUST IN TIME FOR THE CONVENTION. "WE EXCHANGED EMOTIONALLY CHARGED HANDSHAKES…THEN CARRIED THE CANOE ON OUR SHOULDERS TO THE MARRIOTT." WISE AND YORK PLANNED AND EXECUTED THEIR TRIP TO RAISE AWARENESS AND FUNDS FOR THE V FOUNDATION FOR CANCER RESEARCH. THE TWO MEN WERE ON STAGE THREE DAYS LATER TO PRESENT THE FOUNDATION WITH DELTA CHI'S $130,000 CHECK.

Funded by Delta Chi Educational Foundation and Fraternity, the 2010 "A's" Academy was deemed a great success.

DELTA CHI

Quarterly

Winter/Spring 2010

Delta Chi Returns To St. Meinrad
for the 2010 "A"s' Academy!

DELTA CHI
57TH INTERNATIONAL CONVENTION IN NEW ORLEANS, AUGUST 11-15 2010

Ron Mix posed with fellow Southern California brothers at the 2010 convention. From left to right are Joshua Reutter ('11), Andrew Shannon ('11), Ron Mix ('60), Donald LaPlante (Southern California alumnus initiate), and Todd Holmes ('80).

Pat Gillick (Southern California '58) was inducted into the National Baseball Hall of Fame in 2011. Gillick was general manager for the Toronto Blue Jays (1978–94), the Baltimore Orioles (1996–98), the Seattle Mariners (2000–03), and the Philadelphia Phillies (2006–08). His teams were World Series Champions in 1992, 1993, and 2008.

Chapter Thirteen:
The Future of Delta Chi

HANDS ACROSS THE CENTURIES

> *"To me, the future of this very own society of ours has no uncertainties. I do not view it with alarm. I know as the years roll on that this brotherhood of ours will go through wider fields of effort to a finer destiny."*
>
> FOUNDER PETER SCHERMERHORN JOHNSON
> CELEBRATING DELTA CHI'S FIFTIETH ANNIVERSARY

The growth of Delta Chi follows a clearly upward trajectory. The 858 initiates recorded in 1900 would have been shocked to be included in the 101,377 total initiates as of 2010. The similarities between the Delta Chi of yesterday and the Delta Chi of today are more striking than the differences. The tenets of the Preamble remain the bedrock of the fraternity. The history of Delta Chi illustrates the great advantages derived from a brotherhood of college and university men. There are countless examples of lifelong friendships derived from this close association and men of great character do tribute to Delta Chi through their actions every day. With a deep appreciation of the dedicated men who have gone before them, the future of Delta Chi rests in a new generation. In the class of most recent initiates there is one man, whose name will not be known for decades. He will one day be the oldest Delta Chi attending a convention. He will stand, full of pride and Delta Chi devotion, and will say, "With my handshake, I bond you to your brothers of the past. When you are old men, you will stand where I am and will pass my handshake on." There is no doubt that Founder Sweetland's handshake across the centuries will continue to connect Delta Chi brothers long into the future.

Appendix A

Conventions of the Delta Chi Fraternity

Convention	Date	Location
1	1894	Ann Arbor, Michigan
2	1896	New York, New York
3	1897	Ithaca, New York
4	1898	Chicago, Illinois
5	1899	Carlisle, Pennsylvania
6	1900	New York, New York
7	1901	Buffalo, New York
8	1902	Chicago, Illinois
9	1903	New York, New York
10	1904	Ithaca, New York
11	1905	Toronto, Ontario, Canada
12	1906	Ann Arbor, Michigan
13	1907	Washington, D.C.
14	1908	Syracuse, New York
15	1909	Ithaca, New York
16	1910	Columbus, Ohio
17	1911	Chicago, Illinois
18	1913	Toronto, Ontario, Canada
19	1915	San Francisco, California
World War I		
20	1919	Minneapolis, Minnesota

Convention	Date	Location
21	1921	Columbus, Ohio
22	1923	Evergreen, Colorado
23	1925	Glacier National Park, Montana
24	1927	Lake of the Bays, Canada
25	1929	Estes Park, Colorado
26	1931	West Baden, Indiana
no convention	1933	
27	1935	Yellowstone National Park
no convention	1937	
28	1940	Ithaca, New York
World War II		
29	1952	French Lick, Indiana
30	1954	Biloxi, Mississippi
31	1956	East Lansing, Michigan
32	1958	Lake Texoma, Oklahoma
33	1960	Indianapolis, Indiana
34	1962	Colorado Springs, Colorado
35	1964	New Orleans, Louisiana
36	1966	St. Louis, Missouri
37	1968	Chicago, Illinois
38	1970	Dallas, Texas

Convention	Date	Location
39	1973	New Orleans, Louisiana
40	1975	Chicago, Illinois
41	1977	Kansas City, Missouri
42	1979	Iowa City, Iowa
43	1981	Indianapolis, Indiana
44	1983	Nashville, Tennessee
45	1985	Chicago, Illinois
46	1987	New Orleans, Louisiana
47	1990	Syracuse, New York
48	1992	Irvine, California
49	1994	Atlanta, Georgia
50	1996	Dallas, Texas
51	1998	St. Louis, Missouri
52	2000	Phoenix, Arizona
53	2002	Orlando, Florida
54	2004	Washington, D.C.
55	2006	Cleveland, Ohio
56	2008	Las Vegas, Nevada
57	2010	New Orleans, Louisiana
58	2012	Pittsburgh, Pennsylvania

Appendix B

"AA"s

Name	Chapter	Years Served
Owen Lincoln Potter	Cornell 1891	1890 to 1894
Charles A. Park	Michigan 1894	1894 to 1896
Bertrand Lichtenberger	Michigan 1896	1896 to 1897
John E. Amos	Chicago-Kent 1896	1897 to 1898
A. Dix Bissell	Cornell 1898	1898 to 1899
Mark H. Irish	Osgoode Hall 1897	1899 to 1900
Robert R. McKee	NYU 1893	1900 to 1901
Carleton Gillespie Ferris	Michigan '01	1901 to 1902
James O'Malley	Cornell '01	1902 to 1903
A. Frank John	Dickinson '00	1903 to 1904
Edward C. Nettels	Chicago-Kent '00	1904 to 1905
Floyd L. Carlisle	Cornell '03	1905 to 1906
John J. Kuhn	Cornell 1898	1906 to 1907
Harry Hyde Barnum	Chicago-Kent '03	1907 to 1908
Joseph Hartigan	NYU '06	1908 to 1909
Frank W. Atkinson	Michigan '01	1909 to 1910
Ward Wright	Osgoode Hall '08	1910 to 1911
Osmer C. Ingalls	Ohio State '07	1911 to 1913
Henry V. McGurren	Chicago-Kent '10	1913 to 1917
John J. Kuhn	Cornell 1898	1917 to 1921
Henry V. McGurren	Chicago-Kent '10	1921 to 1927
William W. Bride	Georgetown '04	1927 to 1929
John B. Harshman	Ohio State '07	1929 to 1935
Charles M. Thompson	Illinois Faculty	1935 to 1952
Marsh W. White	Penn State Faculty	1952 to 1954

Name	Chapter	Years Served
Jefferson J. Coleman	Alabama '29	1954 to 1956
L. Orville Edlund	Illinois '33	1956 to 1958
Joseph F. Lacchia	NYU '25	1958 to 1960
Lewis S. Armstrong	Washington '39	1960 to 1962
L. Harold Anderson	Stanford '24	1962 to 1964
Claude B. Layfield Jr.	Auburn '46	1964 to 1966
David A. Gillespie	Illinois '27	1966 to 1968
Ralph E. Prusok	Union '52	1968 to 1969
George W. Obear	DePauw '30	1969 to 1970
Frank Granat Jr.	Washington '51	1970 to 1973
James C. Steffan	Ohio State '22	1973 to 1975
Marcus Gary Monk	Auburn '65	1975 to 1977
J. Nick Gray	Missouri '56	1977 to 1979
Robert P. LaBouy	Washington '66	1979 to 1981
Raymond F. Borelli	Illinois '58	1981 to 1985
Fredrick B. Hammert	Oklahoma '60	1985 to 1987
Larry P. Audlehelm	Iowa '71	1987 to 1990
Gregory F. Hauser	Michigan State '75	1990 to 1992
Michael L. Carroll	Auburn '71	1992 to 1994
Larry K. Nothnagel	Truman State '79	1994 to 1996
Paul W. Bohlman	Ohio State '70	1996 to 1998
William A. Williams	Gannon '83	1998 to 2002
Charles A. Mancuso	Florida State '84	2002 to 2004
Steven P. Bossart	Kent State '90	2004 to 2008
Thomas S. Horowitz	Michigan State '87	2008 to 2010
Ratheen C. Damle	Texas '01	2010 to present

APPENDIX C

Delta Chi Chapters

Order	University/College	Location	Date of Chartering (Date Closed)
1	Cornell	Ithaca, NY	1890
2	NYU	New York, NY	1891 (1943)
3	Albany Law - Albany Law School (Reestablished as Union Chapter)		1892 (1894)
4	Minnesota	Minneapolis, MN (Inactive 1943–45)	1892
5	DePauw	Greencastle, IN (Inactive 1894–1928)	1892 (2011)
6	Michigan	Ann Arbor, MI (Inactive 1935–48, 2001–07)	1892
7	Dickinson	Carlisle, PA	1893 (1933)
8	Northwestern	Evanston, IL (Inactive 1909–99)	1893
9	Chicago-Kent	Chicago, IL	1896 (1934)
10	Buffalo	Buffalo, NY (Inactive 1935–79)	1897 (1991)
11	Osgoode Hall - U of Toronto	Toronto, ON, Canada	1897 (1975)
12	Syracuse	Syracuse, NY (Inactive 1917–66, 1970–2004)	1899
13	Union	Schenectady, NY	1901 (1994)
14	West Virginia	Morgantown, WV	1902 (1909)
15	Ohio State	Columbus, OH (Inactive 1983–89, 2003–11)	1902
16	New York Law	New York, NY	1902 (1907)
17	Chicago	Chicago, IL	1903 (1929)
18	Georgetown	Washington, DC	1903 (1943)
19	Pennsylvania	Philadelphia, PA (Inactive 1917–29)	1904 (1949)
20	Virginia	Charlottesville, VA	1905 (1936)
21	Stanford	Palo Alto, CA	1905 (1970)
22	Washington University	Saint Louis, MO	1906 (1909)
23	Texas	Austin, TX (Inactive 1970–89)	1907
24	Washington	Seattle, WA	1908
25	Nebraska	Lincoln, NE	1909 (1953)
26	Southern California	Los Angeles, CA	1910
27	Abracadabra	Berkeley, CA (Inactive 1969–78, 1994–2003)	1910
28	Iowa	Iowa City, IA	1912
29	Kentucky	Lexington, KY (Inactive 1954–75)	1913 (1981)
30	Wisconsin	Madison, WI (Inactive 1949–92)	1921 (1995)
31	Columbia	New York, NY	1923 (1943)
32	Kansas	Lawrence, KS	1923
33	Iowa State	Ames, IA	1923 (2001)
34	Illinois	Champaign, IL	1923
35	Idaho	Moscow, ID	1924
36	Arizona	Tucson, AZ	1925
37	Indiana	Bloomington, IN (Inactive 2002–09)	1925
38	Florida	Gainesville, FL (Inactive 2002–08)	1926
39	Alabama	Tuscaloosa, AL	1927
40	Oklahoma	Norman, OK (Inactive 1961–85, 1990–2012)	1927
41	Purdue	West Lafayette, IN	1927
42	SMU	Dallas, TX	1927 (1985)
43	Penn State	State College, PA	1929
44	Oregon State	Corvallis, OR (Inactive 2000–06)	1931
45	Miami	Oxford, OH	1932
46	UCLA	Los Angeles, CA	1934 (1958)
47	Michigan State	East Lansing, MI	1935
48	LSU	Baton Rouge, LA (Inactive 1953–65, 1966–84, 2002–06)	1941
49	Rollins	Winter Park, FL	1941 (1970)
50	Washington State	Pullman, WA (Inactive 1971–88)	1943
51	Hobart	Geneva, NY	1948
52	Oklahoma State	Stillwater, OK	1948 (2000)
53	Arizona State	Tempe, AZ (Inactive 1971–88, 1997–2003)	1949
54	Lake Forest	Lake Forest, IL (Inactive 1966–97)	1950
55	U-Miami	Miami, FL	1950 (1951)
56	Missouri	Columbia, MO (Inactive 1966–78, 1985–88)	1951
57	Auburn	Auburn, AL (Inactive 1986–90)	1951
58	Lehigh	Bethlehem, PA (Inactive 1998–2011)	1952
59	Western Michigan	Kalamazoo, MI (Inactive 1971–84)	1955
60	Connecticut	Storrs, CT	1955 (2011)
61	Southern Illinois	Carbondale, IL (Inactive 1972–76, 1998–2005)	1955
62	Houston	Houston, TX	1956 (1977)
63	Kansas City	Kansas City, MO	1956 (2003)
64	Wayne State	Detroit, MI	1956 (1974)
65	Ball State	Muncie, IN	1958 (2003)
66	Northern Arizona	Flagstaff, AZ (Inactive 1976–86)	1959
67	Texas Western	El Paso, TX	1961 (1966)
68	Florida State	Tallahassee, FL (Inactive 1972–82)	1961 (1998)
69	Oregon	Eugene, OR	1963 (1971)
70	Mississippi State	Starkville, MS (Inactive 1983–85)	1964
71	Kansas State	Manhattan, KS (Inactive 1981–94, 2008–10)	1964
72	Parsons	Fairfield, IA	1965 (1972)
73	Georgia	Athens, GA (Inactive 1983–98)	1965 (2008)
74	Troy State	Troy, AL	1966
75	Livingston - U of W. Alabama	Livingston, AL (Inactive 2006–11)	1967
76	Fullerton	Fullerton, CA (Inactive 1998–2002)	1967
77	Eastern Illinois	Charleston, IL	1967 (2005)
78	Long Beach	Long Beach, CA	1968
79	Jacksonville State	Jacksonville, AL	1968
80	Valdosta	Valdosta, GA	1968
81	Massachusetts	Amherst, MA	1969 (2002)
82	Gorham State - U of S. Maine	Gorham, ME	1969
83	San Diego State	San Diego, CA	1969 (1996)
84	Oshkosh	Oshkosh, WI (Inactive 1981–86)	1969 (2010)
85	Tri-State	Angola, IN	1969
86	Denison	Granville, OH (Inactive 1997–2003)	1969
87	Whitewater	Whitewater, WI (Inactive 1982–87, 2005–10)	1970
88	Youngstown	Youngstown, OH	1970 (1976)
89	Northern Iowa	Cedar Falls, IA	1970 (2003)
90	Idaho State	Pocatello, ID	1970 (1981)
91	Milwaukee	Milwaukee, WI	1970 (1973)
92	Creighton	Omaha, NE (Inactive 1980–87)	1970 (1995)
93	Cal Poly	San Luis Obispo, CA (Inactive 1973–88)	1970
94	Windsor	Windsor, ON, Canada	1971
95	Northeastern	Boston, MA	1971 (1983)
96	Gannon	Erie, PA	1971
97	Sacramento	Sacramento, CA (Inactive 1973–83)	1971 (2002)
98	Central Missouri	Warrensburg, MO	1971
99	Northwest Missouri	Maryville, MO	1971
100	Embry-Riddle	Daytona Beach, FL	1972
101	West Liberty	West Liberty, WV	1972 (1994)
102	Montevallo	Montevallo, AL	1972
103	Johnstown	Johnstown, PA	1972
104	Georgia Southern	Statesboro, GA	1972
105	Illinois State	Normal, IL (Inactive 1986–90, 2000–05)	1973
106	East Texas	Commerce, TX	1973 (1980)
107	Edwardsville	Edwardsville, IL	1974 (1979)
108	California University of PA	California, PA	1974
109	Missouri Western	Saint Joseph, MO	1976 (1979)
110	Southeast Missouri	Cape Girardeau, MO	1977
111	Marquette	Milwaukee, WI	1977
112	Huntsville	Huntsville, AL	1977
113	Truman State University	Kirksville, MO	1978
114	Jacksonville	Jacksonville, FL	1979 (1986)
115	Columbus	Columbus, GA	1980 (1986)
116	New Haven	New Haven, CT	1981
117	Louisville	Louisville, KY	1982 (1994)
118	Texas Tech	Lubbock, TX (Inactive 1996–2006)	1983
119	Colorado	Boulder, CO (Inactive 1998–2005)	1983 (2009)
120	Augusta	Augusta, GA	1983
121	West Virginia Tech	Montgomery, WV	1983
122	Northern Colorado	Greeley, CO	1984
123	Eastern Washington	Cheney, WA (Inactive 2000–12)	1984
124	Appalachian State	Boone, NC	1986
125	Clarion	Clarion, PA	1986 (1994)
126	New Hampshire	Durham, NH	1986 (1992)
127	Missouri State	Springfield, MO (Inactive 1997–2004)	1986
128	Chico	Chico, CA	1987 (2010)
129	Louisiana Tech	Ruston, LA	1987
130	Texas A & M	College Station, TX	1988
131	Central Michigan	Mt. Pleasant, MI	1988
132	Tarleton	Stephenville, TX	1988
133	Northern Illinois	DeKalb, IL (Inactive 2005–11)	1989
134	Behrend	Erie, PA	1990
135	Clemson	Clemson, SC	1990
136	Kent State	Kent, OH	1990 (2010)
137	North Carolina State	Raleigh, NC	1990 (2002)
138	Hayward	Hayward, CA	1990
139	Montclair	Upper Montclair, NJ	1990
140	Bryant	Smithfield, RI	1990

141	Maryland	College Park, MD	1990
142	Western Ontario	London, ON, Canada	1991 (2001)
143	Frostburg	Frostburg, MD	1991
144	Georgia Tech	Atlanta, GA	1991
145	Edinboro	Edinboro, PA	1991 (1995)
146	Fredonia	Fredonia, NY	1991
147	Elmhurst	Elmhurst, IL	1991 (2000)
148	Virginia Commonwealth	Richmond, VA	1991
149	Reno	Reno, NV	1992 (2006)
150	Virginia Tech	Blacksburg, VA	1992 (2007)
151	Mankato	Mankato, MN	1992
152	Northern Michigan	Marquette, MI	1992 (2000)
153	East Carolina	Greenville, NC	1992
154	Florida International	Miami, FL	1992 (1997)
155	American	Washington, DC	1992
156	Western Illinois	Macomb, IL	1993 (2005)
157	Davis	Davis, CA (Inactive 2002–08)	1993
158	Duquesne	Pittsburgh, PA	1994
159	Texas State	San Marcos, TX	1994 (2009)
160	Old Dominion	Norfolk, VA	1994 (2001)
161	Wyoming	Laramie, WY	1994 (2003)
162	Western Carolina	Cullowhee, NC	1994 (2002)
163	Rowan	Glassboro, NJ	1995 (2010)
164	Memphis	Memphis, TN	1995 (1998)
165	West Chester	West Chester, PA (Inactive 2005–10)	1996
166	Radford	Radford, VA	1997
167	Alberta	Edmonton, AB, Canada	1997
168	New Mexico State	Las Cruces, NM	1998 (2007)
169	Kettering A	Flint, MI	1998
170	Kettering B	Flint, MI	1998
171	UNLV	Las Vegas, NV	1998 (2011)
172	Ferris State	Big Rapids, MI	1999 (2011)
173	Rutgers	New Brunswick, NJ	1999
174	South Florida	Tampa, FL	2000
175	James Madison	Harrisonburg, VA	2001
176	Bowling Green	Bowling Green, OH	2002
177	Stephen F. Austin	Nacogdoches, TX	2002
178	South Dakota State	Brookings, SD	2004
179	Colorado State	Fort Collins, CO	2004 (2011)
180	Pittsburgh	Pittsburgh, PA	2005
181	William and Mary	Williamsburg, VA	2005
182	West Georgia	Carrollton, GA	2005
183	Rhode Island	Kingston, RI	2005
184	Coastal Carolina	Conway, SC	2005
185	Binghamton	Binghamton, NY	2006
186	Cortland	Cortland, NY	2007
187	Hofstra	Hempstead, NY	2008
188	Washburn	Topeka, KS	2008
189	George Mason	Fairfax, VA	2009
190	Marshall	Huntington, WV	2009
191	E. Stroudsburg	E. Stroudsburg, PA	2010
192	Corpus Christi	Corpus Christi, TX	2010
193	Kennesaw State	Kennesaw, GA	2010
194	North Alabama	Florence, AL	2010
195	Wilmington	Wilmington, NC	2011
196	USP	Philadelphia, PA	2011
197	Hamilton	Clinton, NY	2011

Delta Chi Colonies

University/College	Location	Date of Organization
Cincinnati	Cincinnati, OH	2006
Eastern Illinois	Charleston, IL	2008
Massachusetts	Amherst, MA	2008
Florida State	Tallahassee, FL	2009
Sacramento State	Sacramento, CA	2009
Spring Hill	Mobile, AL	2010
Kansas State	Manhattan, KS	2010
Case Western Reserve	Cleveland, OH	2010
Riverside	Riverside, CA	2011
Charlotte	Charlotte, NC	2011
Mississippi State	Starkville, MS	2011

To see a listing of current alumni chapters, please visit www.deltachi.org.
Appendices are current as of July 2012.

APPENDIX D

Executive Directors

O. K. Patton (Iowa '12) part-time 1929 to 1951
Donald G. Isett (Kansas '28) part-time 1951 to 1953
Warren W. Etcheson (Indiana '42) part-time 1953 to 1956
Harold E. Buchanan (Wisconsin '35) 1961 to 1966
Dr. F. Kenneth Brasted (Florida '35) 1967 to 1975
Larry P. Audlehelm (Iowa '71) 1975 to 1979
Raymond D. Galbreth (Missouri '69) 1979 to present

Presidents of the Delta Chi Educational Foundation

Charles M. Thompson (Illinois faculty) 1954 to 1956
Donald G. Isett (Kansas '28) 1956 to 1971
Victor T. Johnson (Purdue '32) 1971 to 1983
Jimmie J. Underwood (Kansas '51) 1983 to 1992
M. Gary Monk (Auburn '65) 1992 to 1997
Frederick B. Hammert (Oklahoma '60) 1997 to 2008
Chad M. Wolett (Arizona State '94) 2008 to 2009
Patrick Weber (Oklahoma '87) 2009 to 2010
Chad M. Wolett (Arizona State '94) 2010 to 2011
James M. Marascio (Bryant '93) 2011 to present

APPENDIX E

Delta Chis of the Year

Henry M. Jackson (Washington '34) 1983
Henry W. Hartsfield, Jr. (Auburn '54) 1984
Peyton N. Rhodes, PhD (Virginia '20) 1985
Otis R. Bowen, MD (Indiana '39) 1986
Charles T. Manatt (Iowa State '58) 1987
Kevin Costner (Fullerton '77) 1988
Raymond D. Galbreth (Missouri '69) 1989
William S. Sessions (Kansas '51) 1990
Herbert G. Klein (USC '40) 1991
Edward A. Kangas (Kansas '66) 1992
Charles Marshall (Illinois '51) 1993
Melvin A. Fisher (Purdue '45) 1994
Thomas W. Glasgow (Michigan State '68) 1995
Forrest E. Hoglund (Kansas '56) 1996
Patrick L. Gillick (Southern California '58) 1997
Samuel R. Johnson (SMU '51) 1998
John L. Melvin, MD (Ohio State '55) 1999
Raoul "Rod" Dedeaux (USC '35) 2000
Chauncey W. W. "Tex" Cook (Texas '30) 2001
James H. Webb (USC '67) 2002
Robert L. Stump (Arizona State '51) 2003
Richard C. Shelby (Alabama '57) 2004
John L. Mica (Florida '67) 2005
James B. Stewart (DePauw '73) 2006
Richard Peck (DePauw '56) 2007
G. D. Spradlin (Oklahoma '41) 2008
Christopher "Ashton" Kutcher (Iowa '00) 2009
Ronald J. Mix (Southern California '60) 2010
Alex Vraciu (DePauw '41) 2011
William Meehan (Jacksonville State '72) 2012

INDEX

About the Author

Annie Miller Devoy, a Hotchkiss, Brown, and
University of Missouri School of Law graduate, is
a freelance writer who specializes in researching
and telling the stories of others. Her own story
has led her to live in Columbia, Missouri, with her
husband Bill and her sons Will and Joe.

PRO

D

IT'S ALL
GREEK
TO ME

UNIVERSITY

D-
M

ME

ARE YO

E AR

ΔX
Rock